LIVING FAITH

Stories from the first 150 years

WESTMINSTER PRESBYTERIAN CHURCH ✦ 1857-2007 ✦ MINNEAPOLIS, MINNESOTA

Colophon

Published on the occasion of the 150th Anniversary, 1857–2007,
of Westminster Presbyterian Church, Minneapolis, Minnesota.

ISBN 1-58296-298-7

About the typefaces: Warnock Pro, ITC Officina Sans, Liorah BT
Editorial reference is The Chicago Manual of Style, fifteenth edition.

Separations, printing and binding by Sung In Printing, Seoul, South Korea.
Supervised by Craig Johnson, Shearson Publishing, Inc., Minneapolis.

Jacket design: Sandy Wolfe Wood
Front cover photo: Susan Gilmore
Half-title page: 1903 Minneapolis atlas. Inset: Bohemian Flats, 1898.
Title page: Susan Gilmore
Back cover: Susan Gilmore

TABLE OF CONTENTS

The church on Twelfth and Nicollet from the office and assembly hall side, 1925.

FOREWORD

Mission Statement

In response to the grace of God through Jesus Christ, the mission of Westminster Presbyterian Church is:

To proclaim and celebrate the Good News of Jesus Christ;

To gather as an open community to worship God with dignity and joy, warmth and beauty;

To nourish personal faith and commitment through study, prayer and fellowship;

To be a welcoming and caring Christian community witnessing to God's love day by day;

To work locally and beyond with our denomination and the larger Christian church; and

To be a telling presence in the city.

Early in Westminster's sesquicentennial year a local men's group invited me to speak on the topic, "The Importance of a Downtown Church." I talked about the history of Westminster's buildings and their three different locations in downtown Minneapolis. I spoke about the pastors of the church and some of Westminster's well-known members. I concluded by arguing that Westminster had helped create the culture of this city and still makes a key contribution to its life.

After I finished, my listeners began asking questions and making comments, but not about the building or the pastors or the famous citizens in our pews. The men, most of whom were older, wanted to tell the stories they knew about Westminster: Stories told them by their parents and grandparents. Stories they remembered from earlier in their lives. Stories that told the story of this old church.

That is what we set out to do in this book: tell stories. Working with a team of lay leaders, the authors decided not to attempt a chronological account of facts about the church and its history. Westminster has three other books written with that in mind. Instead we wanted to sift through the annals of this remarkable congregation's century and a half of life, find good stories of the people and events that inhabit our history, and tell them with narrative and photography.

While Westminster's history does include major figures in the city's past, it is primarily the story of the faithful. Those faithful come in all categories, with an astounding array of backgrounds and experiences. They share one feature: a love of this church and the faith it has nourished in them over the years.

Here we present a collection of their stories. There are more, to be sure. Some of those we have captured in audio interviews available in the church archives. Others are borne along today by members new and old. Some can be gleaned from the three previous history books. And there are some that have not yet happened.

This book is a door through which we walk into the past of this great church. There we will find brave pioneers, pious settlers, industrious mothers, committed citizens, and visionary leaders. We find a church that has expressed its faithfulness to God in many ways over the years, through good times and bad. Westminster has been through a lot in its first 150 years: fire, death, scandal, financial crisis, relocation. The congregation continues to thrive in downtown Minneapolis, where it began in 1857.

This book is also a window through which we look into the future of Westminster, for in these pages we see the direction in which this church is headed. Since its earliest days, basic commitments in our congregational life have not changed all that much. We have kept the worship of God at the center. We have steadfastly remained in the heart of the city. We have welcomed newcomers to Minneapolis. We have encouraged the growth of the Christian church. We have nurtured our children in the faith. We have cared for one another. We have addressed social issues of the day. We have extended ministry beyond the confines of this city. We have shown remarkable resilience.

The Bible uses a range of images to describe the church: a body with diverse parts, a building with Christ as the cornerstone, a family in which all are siblings, a tree bearing good fruit. Those metaphors help us know and understand Westminster. As children many of us learned another image. Remember the old rhyme, said with closed hands, "Here is the church, here is the steeple," and then with open hands and wriggling fingers, "Open it up, and see all the people!"

Open this book, and see all the people. See a band of the faithful who have worshiped God and served Jesus Christ in Minneapolis for 150 years. See their living faith. See the past, and peer into the future.

Then give thanks to God, from whom all blessings flow!

Timothy Hart-Andersen
March 2007

There is a river whose streams make glad the city

of God, the holy habitation of the Most High.

God is in the midst of the city;

it shall not be moved;

God will help it when the morning dawns.

Psalm 46:4-5

A FIRM FOUNDATION

"The leaven of practical Christianity cannot be too abundant in our rushing Western life and our Christianity will be none the worse if it has the flavors of Presbyterianism."

Minneapolis Daily Tribune, May 20, 1886

St. Anthony Falls, ca. 1866

In the foreground of this 1857 view of Minneapolis is a boarding house run by Judith Walsh, where Hiram W. Wagner, Westminster's first tenor soloist, lived in 1860.

A FIRM FOUNDATION

EARLY PRESBYTERIANS IN MINNESOTA

In the spring of 1834 when Minnesota was still "Indian Country" and the only white inhabitants in the region were soldiers, fur traders, speculators, and adventurers, the first Presbyterians arrived at Fort Snelling. Two laymen, Gideon Pond and his brother Samuel, who came on their own initiative from Galena, Illinois, gained permission from the fort's commander to build a small cabin on Lake Calhoun and to teach plowing and farming in a nearby Dakota village. A stream of Presbyterians would soon follow.

A year later the Presbyterian American Board of Commissioners for Foreign Missions sent the first ordained minister, the Reverend T. S. Williamson, also a medical doctor, to gather information for a long-term mission to the region. Williamson returned in May 1836 with a small group from his home presbytery in Ohio. They soon decided that the Fort Snelling soldiers needed mission work as much as the Indians. Aside from these few Presbyterians, there were not yet any Christian clergy or places of worship in the area. Gideon Pond observed in a letter to friends in Connecticut dated February 23, 1835, "I should say there was a revival of religion, but there was none before to revive, and so I will rather say, religion has just begun."

Gaining converts among the rough sorts of men who came to the frontier was challenging, but they gradually gathered a few. Major Gustavus A. Loomis, the commanding officer at Fort Snelling, joined their fledgling Presbyterian Church at St. Peters, named for the river now called the Minnesota, in a little schoolhouse near "Ha Ha Falls." It was reputed to be the first Christian congregation in the Northwest, a region extending from Minnesota to Montana.

Over two decades Williamson established medical missions to the Dakota with major outposts in Lac-qui-Parle in western Minnesota, Kaposia near present-day South Saint Paul, and Pejuhutazizi (Yellow Medicine) near Granite Falls. As white settlers began to arrive in the 1840s, Williamson recruited additional Christians to the region, including the first schoolteacher, Miss Harriet Bishop, who was Baptist, and another Presbyterian minister, the young Reverend Edward D. Neill, who would become one of Minnesota's most influential early figures.

Rev. Neill stepped off a steamboat in St. Paul in the spring of 1849, the same year that the U.S. Congress declared Minnesota a territory. Representing the more liberal New School faction of Presbyterians, he sought to establish the first permanent place of worship in the territorial capital, St. Paul. Neill was disappointed with what he found: "No Lord Baltimore as the presiding spirit—no graduate of the University of Paris, like the founder of Philadelphia—no men of faith and principle, like the settlers at Plymouth Rock." Instead, he saw an "ignoble" crowd, "men of big dreams and slim means." >>>

Presbyterian missionaries first arrived at Fort Snelling in 1834.

Fort Snelling as Concentration Camp

The Dakota's response to the *wasichu,* the strangers moving into their home-land, was remarkably non-violent, even as treaties shrank their lands and Christian missions and other influences eroded their culture. By August 1862 grief and anger compounded by hunger and treaty violations reached an incendiary level. Chief Little Crow was persuaded to lead an attack on the Lower Sioux Agency, igniting a six-week war that spread to farms and towns in the Minnesota River Valley. Government retaliation was harsh and indiscriminate. Thirty-eight Dakota men, several of them Presbyterian converts, were hanged in Mankato in the largest execution in U.S. history. Nearly all Dakota and Ho-Chunk (Winnebago) people were ordered banished from the state. This deceptively beautiful photo shows the camp at Fort Snelling where 1,700 Dakota women, children, and elders were imprisoned through the winter after a forced 150-mile march. Those who survived were deported down the Mississippi River and up the Missouri on overcrowded steamboats.

I should say there was a revival of religion, but there was none before to revive, and so I will rather say, religion has just begun.

Gideon Pond, in a letter to friends in Connecticut, dated February 23, 1835.

>>>
Yet by November he had assembled a small group of men and women into the First Presbyterian Church of Saint Paul, meeting at the Central House on Minnesota Street. Dr. Williamson presided over their first communion services in January 1850, bringing with him a few Dakota women, converts from Kaposia. An Oak Grove Church, later called First Presbyterian Church at Minnehaha, had begun west of the Mississippi River in December 1847 with leadership from Samuel and Gideon Pond, now ordained ministers, and Henry H. Sibley, a prominent fur trader and later the first governor of the state. In the winter of 1849-50 Neill also held services every Sunday afternoon at the Falls of St. Anthony, where he drew a congregation even larger than in St. Paul. This work led to the First Presbyterian Church of St. Anthony, which aligned, like the others, with the New School branch of the church.

Neill's considerable energy also extended to writing. His *Handbook for Presbyterians in Minnesota* (1856) instructed the frontier faithful in Presbyterian history and theology and provided guidance in maintaining a devout life without the benefit of established churches. Among his many other books is a 625-page history of Minnesota, published in 1858, the year of its statehood. His primary passion, however, was for building institutions of higher learning. In 1851 he helped to establish the University of Minnesota, which he served as chancellor. The opening of Macalester College in 1874 fulfilled his longtime dream of a denominational college. Neill became its first president.

Presbyterians' influence on the region in the mid-nineteenth century was remarkable. In 1933, Minnesota's seventy-fifth anniversary year, the *Saint Paul Pioneer Press* noted that no other denomination had sent as much financial support to Minnesota as the Presbyterian Board of Home Missions nor erected as many churches to minister to the men, women, and children on the frontier. ✛

OUR CONGREGATION'S ANCESTRY

Westminster was founded April 23, 1857, by eight people of Welsh and Scottish heritage not content with the theology of First Presbyterian Church, the only Presbyterian congregation in Minneapolis and St. Anthony. Lewis Hudson Williams and his brother Joseph Cloyd were sons of the Reverend Joshua Williams, pastor for twenty-seven years at Big Spring Presbyterian Church in Newville, Pennsylvania. The brothers operated a hardware business and married sisters Tabitha and Sarah McKeehan. A friend on the frontier had written to Lewis encouraging him to move west. In April 1856, no young pioneer at fifty-four, he took a scouting trip to Minneapolis, where land could be had at $1.25 an acre. >>>

Clockwise from top right:
Andrew Oliver (1805-75), founder and first ruling elder of Westminster Presbyterian Church.

The link between Westminster and the Cumberland Valley in Pennsylvania, the birthplace of its original members.

Big Spring Presbyterian Church in Newville, PA, the home church of the two Williams families who founded Westminster.

1849
St. Anthony, on the east side of the Mississippi River, surveyed and platted as a town site

1852
An act of Congress shrinks the Fort Snelling reservation and opens Minneapolis to white settlement

1853-57
Population grows in Minnesota Territory from 40,000 in 1853 to approximately 150,000

1857
Westminster Presbyterian Church founded by eight people of Welsh and Scottish heritage

St. Anthony, at present-day Central and University Avenues, from the roof of the Winslow House hotel, 1857.

Williams left a 120-year-old church to move to a brand new town with no church of his Old School denomination. St. Paul and St. Anthony were bustling, but land on the west bank of the Mississippi had been held by the Fort Snelling Military Reservation until 1855. Lewis bought a house on what is now Second Avenue North in Minneapolis and returned for the family. In June 1856 he and Tabitha and their six children took the train to Pittsburgh to board an Ohio River steamboat. A second steamboat brought them up the Mississippi to St. Paul where the journey continued by wagon. They welcomed Joseph and Sarah and their four children on August 10, 1857.

The next order of business was to charter an Old School congregation with the Presbytery of St. Paul, together with Andrew and Sarah Oliver. We can only guess that Andrew, a Pennsylvania native in his fifties, was the friend who lured Lewis westward. He and Sarah had migrated in stages and prospered by trading land in Illinois. Lewis and Tabitha's adult daughters, Ellen Mary and Deborah, joined them in the charter. Deborah's new husband, Curtis H. Pettit, remained a Quaker yet chaired Westminster's Board of Trustees for fifty-five years until his death in 1913.

Minnesota Territory lay mainly in New School hands, so to keep their allegiance, the Williams brothers had to start a church of their own. They had been raised in a daily, devoutly Calvinist practice of faith. Their father is portrayed in the family's history as "grave, dignified, and solemn, always earnest," a man whose "common practice was to turn the conversation into a higher channel." He reread Jonathan Edwards' *Freedom of the Will* annually. Rev. Williams had planned to send Lewis to college and hoped that he might be called to the ministry, but after another son died at Princeton Seminary, he kept Lewis at home. As Westminster's founder and Clerk of Session, Lewis nevertheless influenced the life and direction of an important emerging church. Congregants called him "mighty in the Scriptures." Joseph kept a lower profile because of frail health.

In midlife Lewis began spelling his name "Louis," to the chagrin of his staunchly Welsh family. Our clearest glimpse into his character comes at a critical moment in the church's history. General Assembly had recommended that the practice of keeping elders active on Session for their lifetimes be replaced with a rotary system. Ordination was forever, but terms on Session would be limited. Westminster adopted this policy in 1878 and conducted an election. Louis Williams, ordained for forty-six years and on Westminster's Session for twenty, was re-elected to a three-year term.

1858
Newspaper promotion of the Minnesota Territory prompts over one thousand steamboat arrivals in St. Paul

1858
Minnesota becomes thirty-second state admitted to the Union of the United States of America

1861
Westminster dedicates its first church home on Fourth Street

At the congregational meeting Joshua Williams read a letter from his father decrying "my summary degradation from the office you entrusted me with, as unkind, unjust, and unlawful treatment." Louis appealed to the Bible and the Confessions of the church to protest the change and declined his re-election "because I regard the tenure of it as without any warrant from Scripture, and necessarily tending to degrade a Divine ordinance to a human expedient." The congregation must have been stunned as "the meeting closed without any formal adjournment."

The intensity of Louis's outrage is cause for speculation. At seventy-six, he was watching the city's wealthy assume leadership of the church. Although materially comfortable, he had modest habits. Life, however, had been rather unkind to Mr. Williams. Shortly after he arrived here, an injury left him virtually blind. Tabitha returned to Newville in 1866 to help her aging parents, died unexpectedly, and lay buried far away. Besides four children lost in childhood, he had outlived two adult daughters. He was mourning the recent deaths of his brother Joseph and a niece and granddaughter, and now his trust in the church he had started was shifting underneath him. He kept his membership at Westminster but began attending First Presbyterian.

Louis Williams was not the only one offended. Elder Isaac McNair and Clerk of Session Charles Vanderburgh also departed for First Presbyterian. Loyal son Joshua Williams, who read the Bible aloud to his father daily, soon followed, as did some

other family members. Ironically, the rotary eldership changed nothing but procedure. When sitting elders' terms expired, they were all re-elected. Those who tried to resign were persuaded to stay.

Louis and Tabitha's daughters Deborah Pettit and Alice Chalmers remained active at Westminster, and other relatives came back after the turn of the century. To this day, Westminster Church counts in its congregation several descendants of our imposing theological forebear, Rev. Joshua Williams. ✛

At left: Founding father Louis Williams (1802-89) was nearly blinded when a tree branch pulled out of his way snapped back and struck him across the eyes. *Above:* After that he held his face close to the paper and wrote his notes for teaching Sabbath school in tiny yet fully legible penmanship.

1862
The Dakota Conflict sweeps up Minnesota River Valley with attacks from hungry Dakota angered by failing land treaties and unfair practices of local traders

1862
Minnesota's first railroad is completed, connecting Minneapolis and St. Paul

WHAT DOES "OLD SCHOOL" MEAN?

These "palpable perversions of religious truth," one Old School partisan asserted, would "introduce upon the American stage the shocking theological panorama of universal derangement and confusion in the elements of the moral world."

Today Westminster's theology tends toward the progressive wing of Presbyterianism, but its founders were distinctly conservative. They belonged to the Old School branch of the Presbyterian Church, which adhered to a strict interpretation of the Westminster Confession of 1646. At Westminster's founding in 1857 nearly all the Presbyterian churches and missions in Minnesota were affiliated with the New School branch.

The Old School/New School conflict started over Presbyterians' relationship with Congregationalists. Historically the two groups envisioned themselves as adherents of a common theological tradition inspired by the Westminster Confession. The Congregationalists settled in New England and Presbyterians in the mid-Atlantic states, but they frequently cooperated with each other. In the colonial period, preachers like the Reverend Jonathan Edwards (1703-58) could move easily between denominations. Born into a Congregationalist family, Edwards studied at Congregationalist Yale, took a post at a Presbyterian church in New York City, later moved among several Congregational congregations in Massachusetts, and finished his days as president of a Presbyterian institution, the College of New Jersey (now Princeton).

The cooperative spirit reached its apex in the 1801 Plan of Union, which brought American Presbyterians and Congregationalists together to establish mission churches in "new settlements." Their union also fostered a "benevolent empire" of interdenominational voluntary organizations such as the American Board of Commissioners for Foreign Missions, the American Bible Society, and the American Home Missionary Society, all of which helped plant churches in Minnesota Territory.

Soon, however, the partnership began to unravel. Groups within each denomination argued vehemently over the nature of sin, atonement, and free will. Conservative Presbyterians rejected the "shocking" practice in some Congregational and liberal Presbyterian bodies of allowing women to lead prayer in "promiscuous assemblies," mixed gatherings of men and women. While neither faction condoned slavery, New School adherents more readily accepted abolition movement activism. Old School Presbyterians opposed radicalism in all its forms. These "palpable perversions of religious truth," one Old School partisan asserted, would "introduce upon the American stage the shocking theological panorama of universal derangement and confusion in the elements of the moral world." In an age when theology was the subject of dinner table conversations, these differences became insurmountable.

Schism was the result. In 1837 General Assembly voted to expel the four New School synods, which clung to the "deranged" ideas. Presbyterians remained divided into separate Old School and New School denominations until 1870. ✦

Above: Rev. Jonathan Edwards' fiery preaching has become an enduring expression of revivalist Calvinist theology in the First Great Awakening.

FIRST MINISTERS

. . . while Iowa and Wisconsin had achieved statehood by 1849, Minnesota was regarded as "a useless tundra, filled with hostile Indians." Only a unique character with a clear sense of mission would thrive on the frontier.

Fine preaching has become a hallmark of Westminster. It wasn't always so. Westminster's first ministers were a sundry lot who came and went in rapid succession. Without a building and unable to offer a decent salary, the tiny congregation found it difficult to attract a preacher. Moreover, while Iowa and Wisconsin had achieved statehood by 1849, Minnesota was regarded as "a useless tundra, filled with hostile Indians." Only a unique character with a clear sense of mission would thrive on the frontier.

The Reverend Benjamin C. Dorrance, a graduate of the Danville Theological Seminary, was the first of Westminster's ministers. He led services for the fledging congregation in a series of borrowed buildings: the Free Will Baptist Church, the Methodist Church, and Fletcher's Hall. Described as a "pleasant and forcible preacher" who "endeared himself to all," Dorrance suffered from feeble health and after just five months returned East and "literally died in his mother's arms." It was an inauspicious start.

Nine months later and still with no replacement, Westminster and St. Anthony (later renamed Andrew) Presbyterian Church agreed to share expenses and together hire the Reverend Levi Hughes, of Logansport, Indiana. He stayed little more than a year. "His sermons were characterized by strength rather than elegance," the Reverend Robert Sample later wrote, drawing on church members' memories. "His oratory reminded his hearers of a rough mountain stream which gathers force as it advances, giving notice of its approach from afar, and overleaping every barrier that lies in its way."

>>>

On March 17, 1861, Westminster's forty-three members dedicated their first church home, a white clapboard building on Fourth Street between Nicollet and Hennepin. This 1865 photo shows Plymouth Congregational Church a block down the street.

At right: The relatively simple interior of the Fourth Street Church.

Below: Fans kept the worshipers as cool as could be. The fan shown here is in the church archives and probably dates from a later period.

>>>

Rev. Hughes's pastoral skills were even less polished, hampered by increasing deafness. "Volume of voice seemed to be entirely beyond his control. His utterance was often loud when it should have been low, indistinct when it should have been forcible." Still, people enjoyed his presence, and new members continued to join. When he announced his decision to leave the ministry due to hearing loss, the women of the church offered to cover his pastoral duties among the sick and elderly if he would continue preaching. He left anyway, in the spring of 1860, and eventually found a job as a financial agent at Hanover College in Bloomington, Indiana.

During his short tenure Rev. Hughes launched Westminster's first building campaign, urging the congregation to undertake the practical and spiritual work necessary to erect their own house of worship. "You may accomplish much by prayer," he encouraged them. "You can pray out the lumber, the mortar, and the stone, and when the material is accumulated you can pray the building up." Funds for the new church came from family and friends back East, members' own contributions, and the Presbyterian Church Extension and Foreign Mission Boards.

On March 17, 1861, Westminster's forty-three members dedicated their first church home, a white clapboard building on the south side of Fourth Street between Nicollet and Hennepin. It stood just a few blocks from the bustling center of town.

The Reverend Robert Strong was the first minister to stay longer than a year. He arrived almost miraculously, the congregants would say, just before winter in 1861. After the outbreak of the Civil War, however, the new church struggled to grow. "It was a seed time rather than a harvest," Robert Sample wrote in his *Historical Sketch of the Westminster Presbyterian Church* (1869).

From its sparse population of few more than 175,000, Minnesota sent nearly 25,000 men to war, and some Minnesota regiments suffered extremely high casualty rates. In 1862-63 Minnesotans faced a more immediate challenge in the Dakota uprising. Threatened with starvation, Dakota warriors took up arms, making refugees of many white inhabitants of the southwest portion of the state. In the ensuing months the majority of Minnesota's volunteer regiments were redirected to the frontier. Despite these disruptions, Minnesota's population continued to grow, reaching 250,000 by 1865.

New arrivals trickled in to the modest Fourth Street church. By 1864 the Reverend Robert Condit had replaced Rev. Strong, and many believed he would be the minister to help their church prosper. The son of an eminent Presbyterian preacher, with a degree from Princeton Seminary, he had impeccable credentials. He also seemed to appeal to the ladies. During his three years of ministry 57 new members joined the church, 45 of them women, a notable accomplishment given the state's gender ratio of 56 percent male to 44 percent female in the 1860s. Condit, too, found that

1868
Rev. Robert F. Sample installed as Westminster's pastor

1878
Rocky Mountain locusts destroy much of Minnesota's wheat crop, forcing farmers to diversify

Minnesota's climate did not agree with him, and opportunities beckoned back East. With no prior warning he submitted his resignation on December 24, 1867, leaving the congregation with "disturbed feelings" and "grave apprehensions." The search for a supply pastor would be difficult in the middle of a Minnesota winter.

Lay leadership sustained Westminster in its first precarious years. During the lengthy periods without a minister, lay members read printed sermons and led the singing on Sunday mornings. They held prayer meetings on Thursday evenings without fail. The congregation was close-knit, and the members looked out for one another. No fickle minister would prevent the church from flourishing. ✛

Rev. Robert Strong was Westminster's first permanent minister, serving from 1862 to 1865. His ministry abruptly ended one Sunday morning when, just moments into his sermon, he suddenly declared with an expression of deep physical pain, "I must stop." He never preached again.

Early Presbyterian Churches in Minneapolis and St. Paul

	Theology	Founded
Presbyterian Church at St. Peter's Fort Snelling/Minnehaha Falls	New School	1835
Oak Grove/First Presbyterian Church at Minnehaha	New School	1847
First Presbyterian Church of St. Paul	New School	1849
First Presbyterian Church of St. Anthony	New School	1849-50
Central Presbyterian, St. Paul	Old School	1852
House of Hope, St. Paul	New School	1855
Oak Grove Presbyterian Church Bloomington	New School	1855
Westminster Presbyterian Church	Old School	1857
Andrew Presbyterian Church St. Anthony	Old School	1857

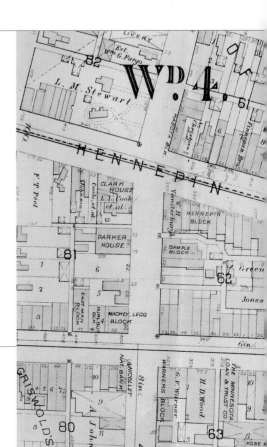

Map at right: The empty lot on 4th Street next to Parker House is where Westminster's first church building stood. The Minneapolis Public Library is across the street now.

MARY CHARLES AND THE DAKOTA CONFLICT

Previous Westminster histories have told the story of music arriving in the person of Miss Mary Charles, who escaped on foot from the Dakota Conflict to become the first organist, playing a little yellow melodeon. Census records help fill out her story.

Mary Charles immigrated from Canada with her family in 1857. Just fifteen, she finished her schooling in New Auburn, Minnesota, where her father operated a gristmill. Her musical gifts won her a job teaching Army officers' children at Yellow Medicine Indian Agency, now the Upper Sioux Agency State Park near Granite Falls.

When word came on August 18, 1862, that some Mdewakanton had attacked the Redwood Agency and killed white people, the Dakota living around Yellow Medicine were divided about how to respond. Some argued that they, too, must kill the whites to protect themselves from retaliation. One who urged caution was John Otherday, who predicted that violence would fill the entire land with U.S. soldiers. Otherday, in his forties, was the leader of the Hazelwood Republic, a community of Wahpeton who farmed in the European style near the Reverend Stephen Riggs's mission. He warned the white people to assemble in safe quarters at the Agency, and just before daybreak he led sixty-two of them across the Minnesota River. It took them five days to reach Shakopee. Otherday told his story of the rescue to the *Saint Paul Press* on August 28, 1862, with Gideon Pond as his interpreter.

How Mary Charles got from the rescue party to Fourth Street and Westminster Church is a missing piece of the story. Once there, she accompanied a choir consisting of Alice Williams and Sophia Emmet, sopranos; Eliza Varney, contralto; Hiram Wagner, tenor and choir leader, and Joshua Williams, bass. By 1870 she had married railroad contractor Neil Graham and left Minneapolis to settle eventually in Owatonna. Widowed at fifty-six, Mrs. Graham lived in the fashion of childless widows of her day, boarding first with her married sister and then in other women's homes. Yet she identified herself to the census taker as the head of her own one-person household. Mary Graham died in 1936 at ninety-four, lauded as "public-spirited" and "talented."

John Otherday joined General Henry Sibley's army of Indian scouts and was awarded $2,500 for his services by the U.S. Congress. He died of tuberculosis at Fort Wadsworth in Dakota Territory in 1869. ✛

Above: John Otherday
At left: The group fleeing Yellow Medicine rests on the prairie.

CHARLES VANDERBURGH

"That many here are devoting their whole time and attention, giving up their body and soul entirely to the acquisition of money, the older they get, is as absurd and foolish as it is wicked. Their benevolence diminishes in proportion as their wealth increases. Happy will it be if they make the discovery before they die that it is all vanity."

Charles Vanderburgh in a letter home to his fiancée, July 6, 1856

Described as a "typical, old-time Presbyterian," Charles Vanderburgh exemplified Westminster's early energetic lay leadership.

Twenty-seven-year-old Charles Vanderburgh arrived in Minneapolis in the spring of 1856 filled with hope, idealism, and youthful energy. An 1852 graduate of Yale College with a law degree in hand, he ignored the advice of friends to settle in Chicago and pressed on for the frontier. Vanderburgh arrived at the right moment. Opportunities abounded for those who worked hard. Within three years he was elected judge of the new Fourth Judicial District, which covered half the state of Minnesota. His reputation was secured by the Eliza Winston case in 1860: A slave who had accompanied her Mississippi owners on their summer vacation at the Winslow House overlooking St. Anthony Falls declared herself free and took refuge with local abolitionists. Vanderburgh ruled in her favor. In 1866 he was elected to the State Supreme Court, where he served for twenty-seven years.

Vanderburgh was also a devoted Presbyterian. He attended First Presbyterian in St. Anthony when he first arrived but soon joined the new congregation of Westminster. His leadership in the church was as energetic as his service to the state. One of his contemporaries called him "a typical old-time Presbyterian Christian. He missed no church services . . . and gave great help both of money and time to the new fields that were being organized as future Presbyterian Churches. He waited for no Home Mission committee or any Board to act. He went ahead and started Sabbath schools and preaching services. [On Sunday] afternoons he distributed tracts and religious papers among the families in the far downtown districts, walking with his basket of religious literature on his arm."

Vanderburgh served Westminster as an elder, Clerk of Session, and superintendent of its Sunday school. When he left the church in 1878 to protest the Session's decision to end elders' life terms, he continued to play a key role in the Presbytery. For twenty years he supervised the Sunday schools at Franklin Avenue Presbyterian, >>>

The Winslow House Hotel, built in 1857 in St. Anthony, was a popular summer vacation spot for wealthy Southerners escaping the heat and humidity. Some brought slaves who, like Eliza Winston, made a break for freedom. When the Civil War slowed tourism, the building found other uses, including as a venue for Macalester College.

>>>

a church he had helped to start. Renamed Vanderburgh Presbyterian Church in 1913, it relocated south of Lake Street on Thirtieth Avenue. (The church was dissolved and the building sold in 1999.)

Vanderburgh's personal life was punctuated by loss. In 1860 he married Julia Mygatt, who succumbed to illness three years later, leaving behind a young son, William Henry, and an infant daughter, Julia. In 1871 nine-year-old Julia also died after falling into the household cistern. Her funeral at Westminster drew hundreds of mourners. Later Charles had a daughter with his second wife, Anna Culbert. Friends described his deep despair when this daughter, too, died tragically, at eighteen.

In 1856 though, this was all in the future. Charles spent his days working as a clerk and his evenings writing letters home to Julia, whom he had left behind in Oxford, New York:

"I wish I were wiser and better and more earnest and faithful. I believe there is less religious enjoyment here than in an eastern society, though it ought not to be so. I am conscious that I fail very much in duty. I feel the need more and more of your dear presence to aid me in living a more holy and consistent life. Everybody, it seems to me, preachers and all, are very worldly here. The spirit of money making and speculating seems to pervade and corrode everything." ✝

November 9, 1856

A leader for Westminster

THE REVEREND ROBERT SAMPLE

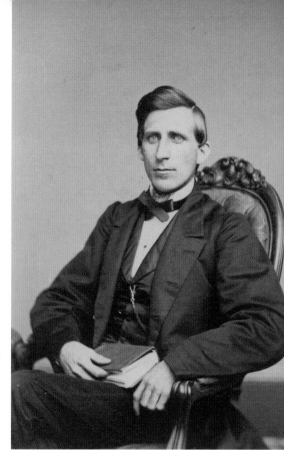

At right: Rev. Robert Sample in his early days at Westminster.

Below: Rev. Robert Sample began the practice of joint Thanksgiving services with Plymouth Congregational Church.

When the Reverend Robert Sample began his ministry at Westminster in March 1868, the congregation prayed that he would stay longer than a year. With God's grace, as his congregants would say, his ministry extended to more than eighteen. Westminster flourished under his leadership. A trustee expressed a common sentiment, "God was better to us than we almost dared to hope."

Keeping him was no easy task. Dr. Sample was never robust in health. He suffered from asthma and hay fever, and his family often fell ill. Several times the church sent him to Colorado and Europe to recuperate. In December 1873 he submitted his resignation with plans to move to "a milder climate" but was forced to reconsider when the St. Paul Presbytery would not let him go.

What he lacked in physical stamina, Dr. Sample more than made up in intellectual vigor. He became one of the best-known ministers in the Northwest, recognized for his passionate preaching and skills for church planting. For many years he chaired the Presbyterian Board of Church Erection, the committee responsible for launching and nurturing new congregations across the United States. Sample also served as a director of the Seminary of the Northwest (later renamed McCormick) in Chicago; a trustee of Macalester College; and a delegate to the Presbyterian Alliance, an international organization that brought Presbyterians together from around the world. His pastoral talents were in high demand, and other churches frequently sought to attract him to their pulpits. Several times he worried the congregation by entertaining job offers elsewhere, but his lifelong commitment to church development led him to remain until 1887.

By that time, Westminster had secured a reputation as the leading Presbyterian church in the region, a distinction reinforced by its hosting of the General Assembly in May and June 1886. Thirteen years later when Westminster again hosted GA, Sample was elected Moderator, the highest position in the Presbyterian Church. He is the only person from Westminster to have achieved that distinction.

Dr. Sample was a forceful and eloquent preacher with an evangelical vision shaped by the ideas of the Second Great Awakening, an American religious revival that began about 1800. Born in 1829 in Corning, New York, and trained at Western Theological Seminary, he honed his preaching skills at the West Twenty-third Street Presbyterian Church in New York City before heading out to Minnesota. "His delivery was slow and deliberate, though sometimes he rose to magnificent bursts of eloquence," Charles T. Thompson, Westminster's Clerk of Session, observed. In his personal demeanor Sample was quiet and modest, although some described him as "severe." One observer

>>>

Rev. Robert Sample boldly waded into current cultural debates, tackling head-on such controversial topics as geology, Darwinism, and higher criticism of the Bible. In February 1876 he launched a minor culture war in Minneapolis with his sermon "Triumphs of Christianity," reprinted in the *Minneapolis Daily Tribune* and circulated in pamphlet form at local newsstands. His confident assertion that Christianity trumped science irritated local members of the National Liberal League, an organization devoted to the separation of church and state. In response, the NLL accused Sample of narrow Christian bigotry and sponsored a public gathering to refute his claims. It is easy to see why they were upset. At a time when geological discoveries and evolutionary theory were challenging the foundations of "truth", Sample clung to a firm belief that Christianity held the answers, however inscrutable. No other religion had spawned such cultural achievements, he argued, and all claims of knowledge stemmed from Christian wisdom.

NATURAL SELECTION.

Above: Caricature of Charles Darwin.

>>>

remarked that he was "without vision in material things of the world," with little appreciation for "the clang of industry, the hum of commerce."

Cultural literacy and intellectual passion were his gifts to the congregation. Sample's love of European cultural traditions shone from the pulpit, and each sermon offered a lesson in history, literature, philosophy, and theology. His references ranged from William Shakespeare to William Cowper, Dante to Darwin, John Knox to John Calvin. In 1870, just two years after his arrival, the Session granted him a six-month paid leave of absence for a European grand tour, an investment he returned handsomely in the years to come. Sample served as a conduit of culture and learning, yet also fearlessly proclaimed the Gospel to a population often sorely tempted by individualism, worldliness, and greed.

His theological vision was notably conservative. While other nineteenth-century evangelicals like Charles Finney, Lyman Beecher, and Francis Asbury experimented with new forms and ideas, Sample stuck close to the Calvinist heritage. He preached passionately about the awfulness of sin and humans' incapacity for goodness. He argued that Christianity should be the basis of civil government. He believed that God had blessed America and orchestrated western settlement. Yet Sample was not narrowly sectarian. He welcomed new members from many denominational backgrounds, working "quietly, but surely" to educate them "until he had developed a united congregation, loyal to the denomination with which it was affiliated." ✣

"A little more than a decade ago there was but a little hamlet where this city of twelve thousand now stands. With manufacturing facilities perhaps unsurpassed on the continent, with agricultural resources of no ordinary kind, with people intelligent, bold, and enterprising, the dual cities at the falls of St. Anthony are destined to wield a power and perform a mission of great and growing importance. For temporal blessings we praise the Lord. Ours is a goodly land, a pleasant heritage."

Rev. Robert Sample, *A Historical Sketch of Westminster Presbyterian Church,* a sermon preached March 14, 1869.

Westminster Trustee William Hood Dunwoody (1841-1914).

If William and Kate Dunwoody were worshiping at Westminster today, what would they do?

Westminster's vitality has long been conjoined with the city's welfare, a fact evident in the Gilded Age of the late nineteenth century. In 1868 a group of local entrepreneurs including bankers H.G. and J.K. Sidle, current and future Westminster trustees, bought the St. Anthony Falls Water Power Co., which had languished under outside ownership. The historian Lucile Kane reports, "When news of the sale was announced, the noise of cannon, steam whistles, and church bells sounded in a 'jollification' celebrating the change in ownership of the company which controlled the city's destiny." Flour mills sprouted along the river banks, joining the sawmills that turned Minnesota's white pine into lumber. Future trustee William Hood Dunwoody persuaded British bakers to import Minnesota's flour, and new railroads brought spring wheat from across the Midwest to meet the demand. Between 1860 and 1870 the value of local manufactures grew from $357,900 to $6,810,970. A good share of that money wound up in the accounts of Westminster members.

The historian Charles Rumford Walker claimed, "Farm boys or young professional men arriving from the East in their twenties frequently found at sixty that they had made three or four fortunes instead of one." Trustee Curtis H. Pettit outdid even that measure, drawing his wealth from banking, real estate, hardware, lumber, newspaper publishing, flour, railroads, and iron ore. A contemporary portrait of W. H. Dunwoody maintains, "He has the faculty of accumulation, with no sordid stain of greed." Resisting greed became a matter of conscience for pious and newly rich Presbyterians. Some of their wealth landed in the collection plate and raised the prospects of "the aristocratic little church" on Fourth Street, as the *Minneapolis Journal* later dubbed Westminster. Their Christian faith required that a portion of their wealth benefit others.

A decade before Scottish American steel magnate Andrew Carnegie wrote "The Gospel of Wealth," prominent Westminster members helped establish a tradition of philanthropy and public service for which Minneapolis is still noted. C. H. Pettit served on the City Council and spent four terms in the state House of Representatives and five in the Senate. He funneled his money into favorite projects without fanfare, served on their boards, and >>>

William Hood Dunwoody's

Last Will and Testament

Dunwoody Industrial Institute, Minneapolis	$ 2,000,000
Minneapolis Society of Fine Arts	$ 1,000,000
Trustees of Westminster Church, Minneapolis	$ 175,000
Minneapolis Young Men's Christian Association	$ 50,000
Minneapolis Woman's Boarding Home	$ 1,000
Presbyterian Board of Relief for Ministers	$ 100,000
Presbyterian Board of Home Missions	$ 100,000
Presbyterian Board of Foreign Missions	$ 100,000
Dunwoody Home for Convalescents, Newtown Farm, PA	$ 1,050,000
Merchants' Beneficial Association, Philadelphia. PA	$ 10,000
Newtown Burying Ground, PA	$ 5,000
Merchants' Fund, Philadelphia	$ 10,000
TOTAL	**$ 4,601,000**

To his family and friends he bequeathed as follows:

To Mrs. W. H. Dunwoody	$ 1,500,000
Three nieces, $150,000 each	$ 450,000
Other relatives, friends, and associates	$ 252,000
TOTAL	**$ 2,202,000**

($1.00 in 1914 equals $20.55 in 2007, according to the online Consumer Price Index Calculator of the Minneapolis Federal Reserve Bank)

>>>

enlisted Westminster members to help. He was most enthusiastic about his work with delinquent boys in the effort that produced the Red Wing Reformatory. He kept a notebook with names and family data, visited the boys' homes, and monitored their progress, serving some as a surrogate father.

Pennsylvania-born William Hood Dunwoody made his fortune in milling, banking, and railroads. Pettit is no longer a famous name, but Dunwoody turns up in arts, educational, and medical institutions. Belief in the character-building virtues of work and the value of a trained work force led him to fund a vocational training school within the public school system. After his death in 1914 it became the freestanding Dunwoody Institute, intended to "provide for all time a place where youth without distinction on account of race, color or religious prejudice, may learn the useful trades and crafts, and thereby fit themselves for the better performance of life's duties." His wife, Kate Dunwoody, encouraged him to build a

hospital for her physician, Dr. Amos Abbott. Dunwoody stipulated that it be turned over at his death to Westminster's Board of Trustees and that two beds be designated for the free use of needy members of Westminster and its mission chapels.

Philanthropy did not demand self-denial. The Pettits and Dunwoodys and other Westminster elite lived in mansions so huge that they required a staff of servants and were identified by name on city maps. The homes were too lavish to survive the economic turns the country has taken since. Present-day worshipers heading home along First Avenue to Highway 394 drive over the ghostly footprints of the W.W. McNair and Eugene Wilson mansions on erstwhile Hawthorn Park.

While philanthropy bridged the gap between rich and poor, it was not meant to close it. The benefactors did not always welcome their beneficiaries' attempts to improve their own lot. Those whose milling companies owned grain elevators in rural areas of the Midwest did not take kindly to farmer cooperatives, nor were they pleased to see unions organize their employees.

The Dunwoody name lives on in a new manifestation: the Dunwoody Crew, a group of homeless people who share accommodations and supplies under the freeway interchange near the Dunwoody Institute. They solicit money from drivers approaching downtown on Dunwoody Boulevard in view of the crest of Lowry Hill where the Dunwoody Mansion once stood. If William and Kate Dunwoody were worshiping at Westminster today, what would they do? ✛

The home of Curtis H. and Deborah Williams Pettit on the southeast corner of Tenth Street and Second Avenue South, now the site of a parking ramp.

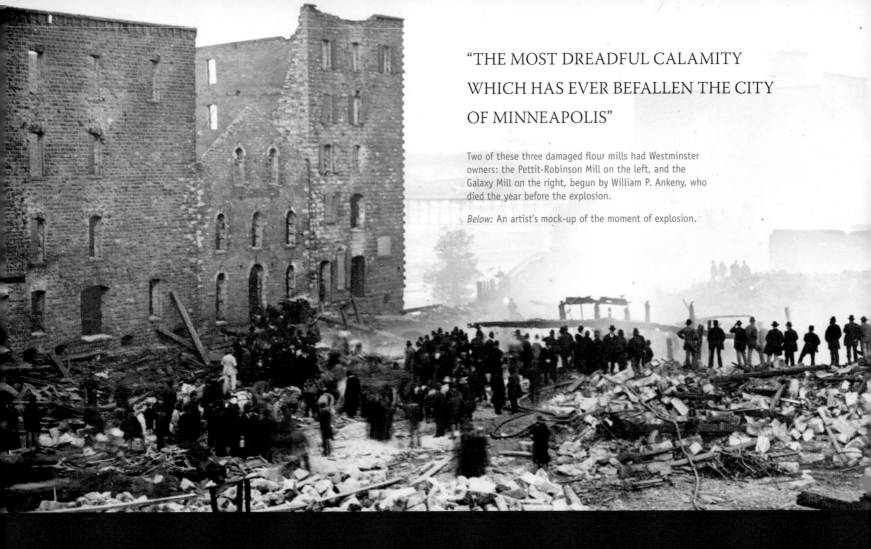

"THE MOST DREADFUL CALAMITY WHICH HAS EVER BEFALLEN THE CITY OF MINNEAPOLIS"

Two of these three damaged flour mills had Westminster owners: the Pettit-Robinson Mill on the left, and the Galaxy Mill on the right, begun by William P. Ankeny, who died the year before the explosion.

Below: An artist's mock-up of the moment of explosion.

Within two decades after Minneapolis opened for settlement it became "the Mill City." The riverfront north of St. Anthony Falls was lined with sawmills, and eighteen flour mills crowded onto the west bank south of the falls. The largest of them, touted as the largest in the world, was the Washburn A Mill at Seventh (now Park) Avenue and Second Street. At 7:20 p.m. on May 2, 1878, a cloud of flour dust inside the Washburn A ignited, causing an explosion so loud that tremors were felt as far away as Stillwater. Fourteen Washburn workers and four in other mills were killed—fewer casualties than had it happened on the day shift. One-third of the milling district lay in ruins. None of the victims belonged to Westminster, but several of the mill owners did.

Westminster officers Curtis H. Pettit, owner of the badly damaged Pettit Mill; lawyer Eugene M. Wilson, the first mayor of Minneapolis after its merger with St. Anthony in 1872; and Surveyor General H. H. Brackett served on the five-man board of the Washburn Mill Disaster Relief Fund. Mill employees donated one day's labor and the owners gave "an equal amount." Fundraisers, including a performance of a musical revue, "Above the Clouds," expanded the resources. Faithful to the paternalism of nineteenth-century charity, the board doled the money out in increments of $25 to $500 to six widows "left destitute and without other sources from which they may expect aid." The fund paid off Mrs. Schei's mortgage and helped Mrs. Savage pre-empt 160 acres near Benson, but when the title fell through, she repaid the money. In January 1880 the balance of $485.23 was divided among seven survivors.

The explosion took a toll on Westminster, too, slowing down the fundraising campaign toward the new church the congregation planned to build. ✝

A Child's View of the Church

Augusta Starr fondly recalled her Sunday school days in the Seventh Street building:

"It was a square building with a tower at each corner in which one could ascend by easy stairs to the auditorium on the second floor. Downstairs on the ground floor was the Sunday school room, surrounded by classrooms, and when they were closed off with folding doors, it was necessary to light the gas in the main room.

"The primary room was even more unique, for it was equipped with rising tiers . . . like circus seats. Timid children clung to the bottom seats while the adventurous ones climbed higher and higher, but every child had an unobstructed view of our teacher, Mrs. Pomeroy. The collection was gathered in a velvet bag at the end of a pole and we sang:

Hear the pennies dropping,
Listen as they fall.
Every one for Jesus,
He will get them all.

But I fear He didn't, for many a penny fell through in the open spaces between the seats, and we remember that two little girls hid their pennies in the lace ruching of their bonnets."

From a talk entitled "Yesterday," given at the Women's Association Luncheon celebrating the 100th anniversary of Westminster, May 1957.

1874
Macalester College founded by Rev. Edward Duffield Neill

1878
Washburn Mill explosion kills eighteen

1878
Construction begins on new church home at Seventh Street and Nicollet

1883
Dedication of Westminster's new church at Seventh Street and Nicollet

1886
Westminster hosts the Presbyterian General Assembly, the first time so far west

Trials and frustrations

THE SEVENTH STREET CHURCH

When the congregation launched its first major capital campaign in 1875 for the construction of a new church building, no one knew what frustrations lay ahead. Initial subscriptions gathered in the first year ranged from ten cents to $2,000 and totaled $30,645.60, enough to boost hopes that the building might be completed within two years. Yet the Board of Trustees proceeded cautiously. With vivid memories of recent deficits and keen knowledge of the tenuous nature of wealth in a boomtown like Minneapolis, they delayed building to debate sites and plans. Eight years later on March 11, 1883, the edifice at Seventh Street and Nicollet Avenue was finally dedicated.

The congregation had to make do in the meantime. By 1879 members outnumbered pews in the Fourth Street building, making Sunday services uncomfortable. The Session acknowledged "the great harm that is done our church by every week's delay in completing our new building. In our visiting we find members of this church who never come here to service and they give as the only reason . . . that they cannot obtain sittings and feel like Trespassers when they occupy someone else's seats and crowd them out." Tempers flared over the lengthy process. Charles T. Thompson, newly elected Clerk of Session, lamented, "We have not had the gracious outpouring of God's spirit among us which we so much longed and prayed for." In a private letter to his fiancée, Kate Harris, he was more pointed: "If there were as much religion as money in the Board of Trustees the church would be finished by this time."

The capital campaign finally ended after Dr. Sample made a special appeal from the pulpit in June 1881. $13,500 came in on a single day. The final cost of the Seventh Street building, first estimated at $40,000, reached nearly $150,000, but the church was dedicated "practically debt-free."

The wait had been worth it. Westminster's new building was hailed as a marvel and proved an attraction to new congregants. Within six years membership rolls had swelled to more than one thousand, spurring the Trustees to consider yet another campaign for expansion. ✛

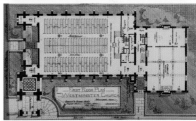

Above: This hand-colored engraving from *American Architect and Building News,* July 29, 1876, depicts plans for a new church at Sixth and Hennepin later abandoned as too expensive.

Far left: A Nicollet Avenue streetscape shows the actual church at Seventh Street, which was designed by the architectural firm Randall & Miller of Chicago and dedicated in March 1883.

Near left: An 1884 lithograph of the Seventh Street church printed to illustrate the use of Minnesota's Fond du Lac brown sandstone. It hangs in the Founders dining room.

"I AM SORRY, SIR, THAT SEAT IS RESERVED."

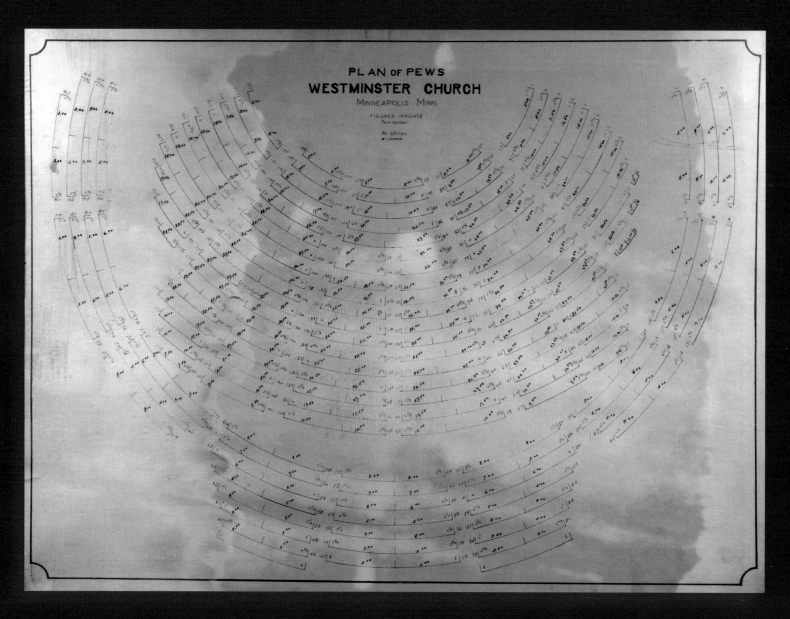

An undated pew rental chart for the Twelfth
Street church, probably from the 1930s. The
system of pew rentals continued until 1956.

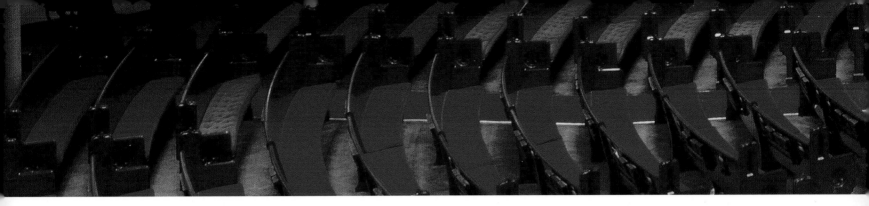

Until 1956 when the pew rental system was finally abandoned, ushers at Westminster faced a delicate task each Sunday morning as they tried graciously to make room for visitors. Members had already rented most of the seats.

The pew rental system was introduced in 1878 to stabilize the budget. In its early years the church relied on voluntary tithing boosted by strongly worded sermons and simply made do with what landed in the offering plate. Chronic under-funding was the result. When the congregation began to plan in earnest for its new, grand church home on Nicollet and Seventh Street, the Trustees took steps to ensure an ample budget. The result was an elaborate system of pew rentals, a common practice in churches at the time.

The first pew rental auction was held on January 25, 1878, at a congregational meeting. After Rev. Robert Sample's family chose their pew (number 53), a professional auctioneer opened the bidding. The Trustees set minimum prices to assure a balanced budget, but then market forces took over. People competed for choice spots, driving up the prices. "Bidding was spirited and resulted in the sale of about two-thirds of the pews," Allen Hill, secretary for the Board of Trustees, reported. Thereafter, pew auctions were held annually and renters were expected to pay their dues quarterly.

The budget stabilized almost immediately. In 1881 pew rentals provided the church a working budget of nearly $4,000 per year. When the Seventh Street building made far more pews available for sale or rent, the auction raised more than $9,000 annually, allowing the church to establish a professional music program and pay its minister a higher salary.

Social winnowing was an unfortunate result. The system assured members of means prime locations. Everyone knew the seat of E. M. Wilson, one of the city's most prominent lawyers, or C. H. Pettit, Chair of the Board of Trustees and mill owner. In 1889 the best seats cost at least $122 a year, while "opera chairs" in the gallery could be had for $5 to $8. Strangers were offered the less desirable seats unless, by some lucky chance, a regular member did not appear. The general rule was that a pew unoccupied ten minutes after the start of the morning service could be given to another person. Seating during evening services was more flexible.

A *Minneapolis Daily Tribune* reporter writing in 1889 believed the system worked, thanks to the hospitality of Westminster's ushers: "In a church so largely attended as Westminster, the greatest care must be taken, on the one hand, to make the stranger at home, and on the other, to preserve the rights of the pew-holders . . . . It is the principle of the church that rich and poor be met with the same welcome, and when they have been ushered to their seats, the Sunday light falling through the stained glass windows over them, as they sit side by side, softens and blends the outlines and figures, making the laborer and the capitalist, the lady and the maid almost indistinguishable to the casual glance of the observer." ✦

A pew rental receipt signed by longtime Westminster treasurer John Ankeny.

From the moment that organist Mary Charles found her way to Westminster, music has infused our congregation with praise and thanksgiving. Changing tides of taste, belief, and practice have added variety to Westminster's musical offerings, but not always to cries of appreciation.

Deep convictions about music are integral to the Reformed tradition. The sixteenth-century Geneva reformer John Calvin warily observed the power of music to lead people closer to God or to lure them into lasciviousness. To counter music's secular tendencies, Calvin emphasized the Word of God as the sole basis for faith and favored congregational singing that drew its lyrics from Scripture. Early Reformed churches often banned musical instruments from worship and restricted singing to psalms.

Practices had loosened by the time Westminster began, but the simplicity remained. Early songbooks used at

the church included both psalms and hymns by such composers as Isaac Watts, Charles Wesley, and Ann Taylor, but they offered only words, not harmonies. For the congregation's first four years, worshipers sang without musical accompaniment and from memory, unless they purchased their own hymnals. Joseph Williams set the pitch with a tuning fork. The small yellow melodeon that Mary Charles played supported the first choir, a quartet plus two additional sopranos. Music sustained these pioneers. Their only disagreement was over when to sit and stand. After long discussions in 1875 the Session agreed worshipers would stand during opening and closing hymns and sit during the long prayer, a practice that continues today.

The music program grew more professional with the move to the Seventh Street building, where the acoustics were considered the finest in the city. Expanded income from pew rentals provided funds to invest in trained musicians. In December 1882 the Trustees increased the music allotment from $150 to the princely sum of $1,600—nearly one-sixth of the church's budget—for an organist, four soloists, and choir director. Borrowing a practice fashionable in New York churches, they established a quartet, rather than a full chorus, and hired an inventive organist and choir director from the East, Professor H. G. Proctor. "In his jovial form and demeanor," the *Tribune* declared, Proctor was "not the foreign musician with long hair and classic phiz, but a new world musician who can see music in other things than strings and pipes, and the human voice."

An 1841 Sunday School hymnal found buried in Westminster's archives.

The acoustics of the Seventh Street church, which featured a magnificent walnut-encased organ, were deemed among the best in the country.

Magnificent organ playing became a defining feature of Westminster's services after Proctor's arrival. While Europe's great churches had long resonated with the sounds of Bach and Buxtehude, organ music became popular in the United States only in the nineteenth century when wealthier churches in the East acquired organs, often imported from overseas. These impressive instruments supported congregational singing, allowed virtuoso performances, and confirmed the congregation's good taste. The Universalists acquired the first organ in Minneapolis, and Plymouth Congregational had one by 1869. Not to be outdone, Westminster's women raised money for an organ but handed over their cache when funds for the new building got tight. By some miracle Westminster was still able to install a notable three-manual organ in the new church.

Nearly every church organization opened its meeting with some favorite tune. The Woman's Home Missionary Society joined in songs still familiar today: "I Love to Tell the Story," "Nearer My God to Thee," "Come Thou Fount of Every Blessing," "Take My Life and Let It Be." Gospel songs came to Westminster in the 1880s and remained a staple well into the twentieth century. Children grew up singing the enormously popular tunes of Dwight L. Moody and Ira D. Sankey, which introduced a brisker pace and livelier rhythms. When the British musical evangelist Gipsy Smith came to Westminster in 1909, the church purchased hundreds of his songbooks, and many joined a new interdenominational chorus called the Gipsy Smith Singers.

These lighter tunes were not without critics. Musical innovations prompted arguments over the right balance between sacred and secular music in worship and Sunday school. One Presbyterian psalmody committee urged churches to sanction "nothing but the best sacred music, rigidly excluding all the light, irreverent rants in which many delight." Westminster's Session tended to agree. After hearing complaints about the music enjoyed by the youth of the church, Session resolved in 1902 "that in all the Sunday Schools of the Church the music, both instrumental and vocal, be confined to the songs and hymns of the Church and such other music generally recognized as sacred music."

Poor musical performances and bad behavior in the choir prompted the Session to take action in 1911. The trouble began when news leaked that the quartet's tenor was living in adultery. He was promptly dismissed. Then Session admonished the choir to select music that would "harmonize with the general spirit of the service and of the particular occasion." Evidently the choices remained unsatisfactory, for the following year Session sacked the whole quartet plus the organist, retaining only Mr. Harry Phillips as music director. Phillips was instructed to select a "competent" quartet and twelve additional chorus members, each of whom would be paid a small salary and expected to behave morally and professionally.

To avoid "a distracting display of millinery in the choir loft," the choir also began wearing robes.

Phillips restored the choir to worthy status and set it to performing concerts, beginning with several performances of Brahms's *A German Requiem*, one a benefit for Belgian war victims. ✦

GENERAL ASSEMBLY 1886

Above: Westminster hosted or served as a venue for General Assembly in 1886, 1899, 1945, 1968, and 1986 and is making plans to host again in 2010.

Below: Delegates to GA in 1945 gather on the front steps of the Twelfth Street building.

Nearly a thousand Presbyterians traveled to Minneapolis in May 1886 for twelve days of General Assembly meetings, the first time the Assembly had been held so far west. The commissioners came from east and west, Asia and Africa, and the various American states. Hotels were bursting, and many Westminster members opened their homes to the visitors. Their presence was considered a great honor both for the congregation and for Minneapolis, a sign of Westminster's stature in the denomination and of the city's ascendance as a center of commerce and culture.

A letter to the *Minneapolis Daily Tribune* signed "not a Presbyterian" urged that "we do everything possible to advertise Minneapolis" to these "distinguished visitors," who are "the leading and prominent businessmen and also of the best culture and thought of the country." Indeed, the *Tribune* deemed the Presbyterian guests important enough to warrant front-page coverage throughout the first week of the gathering.

Rev. Robert Sample's name came up several times as a favorite for the position of Moderator of General Assembly, even though he was ultimately edged out by the Reverend David C. Marquis, a professor of New Testament at the Seminary of the Northwest. Sample cared deeply about many of the issues on the agenda and had nurtured interest in them at Westminster. Home missions dominated, including Sunday schools, missionary work among Indians and the Chinese, and support for Southern freedmen and women. Newly established Macalester College, on whose board Sample served, also garnered much favorable attention.

The Twin Cities' Protestant community was drawn into the events. Presbyterian churches on both sides of the Mississippi hosted special gatherings and ecumenical prayer meetings. Visiting Presbyterian preachers filled the pulpits of Baptist, Methodist, Congregational, Episcopal, Unitarian, Universalist, and YMCA congregations on the first Sunday of the Assembly.

It was the high tide of Presbyterianism in the United States. With all branches of the "family" included—Presbyterian Church in the U.S.A. (PCUSA), Southern Branch, Cumberland Presbyterian, United Presbyterians, and Reformed Churches—the assembled delegates could give thanks for more than fourteen thousand congregations across the country. Only the Baptists and Methodists rivaled them in numbers. ✝

AT WORK IN THE WORLD

"I know thy works: behold, I have set before thee an open door, and no man can shut it; for thou hast a little strength, and hast kept my word, and hast not denied my name." Revelation 3:8

"The open door was for this church—a Missionary church indeed!"

Mrs. E. F. Pomeroy, Woman's Home Missionary Society president, reflecting on Revelation 3:8

National missionary publications kept Westminster women informed about new programs and connected with their counterparts elsewhere.

"Christ's work is women's work" was the oft-repeated motto of the Woman's Home Missionary Society (WHMS), formed in March 1882. Women's mission societies arose across the United States after the Civil War and blossomed with new interest in education and missions on America's borderlands. Money, time, and vision helped to bring schools, churches, and hospitals to Alaska, Utah, Puerto Rico, the Spanish-speaking people of the Southwest, freedmen and mountain people of the South, and immigrants in America's cities.

Westminster's women may have been following others' examples, but their generosity set them apart. In June 1887 the Presbytery of St. Paul was "the banner presbytery" in raising mission funds, with Westminster setting the pace. This outstanding record of mission giving continued for decades.

The Woman's Home Missionary Society and the Woman's Foreign Missionary Society (WFMS) were the pillars of Westminster's outreach in the late nineteenth century. Their combined intake approached the level of the general operating budget. In 1888, for example, the WFMS raised $3,633 and the WHMS, $2,643, while pew rentals, the main source of church income, drew around $9,000. Women's enthusiasm for missions spilled over onto Westminster's youth, with mothers promoting the Young Ladies' Missionary Society and the Boys' Missionary Brigade for their daughters and sons.

While women could neither vote, preach, nor run for office, they wielded a powerful tool, their moral authority. WHMS women envisioned themselves as missionary agents on the frontier, where the battle between sin and salvation was waged visibly and daily. The WHMS secretary reflected on their challenges in 1885: "Since the completion of our great railroad lines—the Northern and Union Pacific—the great barriers which nature had thrown up to separate the east from the west had been annihilated and it lies invitingly open to

1882	1882	1882	1883	1891	1892
Hope and Riverside Missions established by Westminster	Edmunds Act outlaws polygamy; more than 1,300 Mormon men imprisoned	Chinese Exclusion Act curtails further immigration from China	Northern Pacific Railroad completes its transcontinental route from Minnesota to the Pacific	Bureau of Immigration established; Congress adds health qualifications to immigration restrictions	Ellis Island replaces Castle Garden as the New York entry point for immigrants

all—attracted by the inducements offered by land agents, who represent it as a perfect paradise, thousands flock from the east every year—besides the mass exodus from foreign shores. Who can measure the influence which this multitude will have upon our country? Many of those are wicked men, others have been religiously trained but . . . are led astray before they are aware . . . . May God help us to go in and possess the land for Him."

Minneapolis may have felt like the edge of civilization, but frequent letters, missionary publications, and a stream of visitors kept Westminster's women well connected and up-to-date. Many avidly read *The Home Missionary,* a publication of the American Bible Society, and *The Home Mission Monthly* of the PCUSA. Visitors came from Utah, New Mexico, Pennsylvania, Tennessee, and Alaska to speak about Presbyterian women's work among the Mormons, Native Americans, freedmen and poor whites in the South. In 1883 a Rev. Creswell visited from Pembina in Dakota Territory to share news about Presbyterian missions on the northern frontier. He hoped to raise money for a library "to counteract the evil influence of the Saloons and vile Literature that floods their city." In 1885 Miss Josie Bly, a student at Fisk University, spoke about the needs among former slaves. Just months after the Civil War ended, the PCUSA had joined with other Protestant denominations to establish Fisk University as an educational mission to freedmen and women. W. E. B. Dubois graduated from Fisk in 1888, and Booker T. Washington later sat on its Board of Trustees. WHMS donations supported Fisk's growth.

Missions to Native Americans were a special focus. As early as 1837 Stephen and Mary Ann Riggs began work among the Dakota, and Presbyterian missions soon dotted the western landscape. WHMS support went to the Sisseton Agency, where Mary Riggs Morris ran a mission and boarding school. In 1883 the WHMS began to sponsor a ten-year-old boy from the Legunas tribe in New Mexico who attended a Presbyterian mission school in Albuquerque. Originally named Toiku, he was renamed Gaylord Steele after a Westminster boy who had died. Curious about his intellectual fitness, the women asked to see his schoolwork. To their surprise and pleasure, they found "it compares favorably with pupils of the same age in our own city." WHMS sent Gaylord boxes of clothes and books every few months.

Women's unique concerns also drew their attention. The Mormon practice of polygamy, in the national spotlight in the 1880s, provoked them to launch a letter writing campaign to newspapers and elected representatives. The effect of alcohol on family welfare disturbed them. When the Women's Christian Temperance Union held its national convention in Minneapolis in October 1886, Westminster women eagerly joined the throng. They saw the WCTU as "standing at the forefront of reform throughout the length and breadth of the land."

Despite good intentions, WHMS women were not free of prejudice. They reacted with alarm to the rising tide of immigration from Eastern Europe and Asia. An August 1887 article on "Our Immigrant Population" in *The Home Missionary* reported startling statistics about the thousands of immigrants arriving each day at Manhattan's Castle Garden, the official entryway before >>>

Entered at the Post-Office at New York as Second-Class Matter.

NEW YORK, MAY, 1886.

Editorial Notes.

Debt, $139,708.67

HOME MISSIONS, - - $110,170.66
WOMAN'S WORK, - - 29,538.01

"*Resolved,* That this assembly request each church to take a special collection or adopt such other measures as shall seem best in each case to cancel these debts before October next, and before August 1 in every church finding it practicable, leaving it to each contributor to designate his choice of boards, and to each session to apportion undesignated contributions.

"The Assembly hereby appoints one to urge his Presbytery to do what it deems its full share in lifting the pending debt of the Board."

GENERAL ASSEMBLY, 1885.

Sheldon Jackson

Women's home missions owe much to the persistent wrangling of the Reverend Sheldon Jackson, famed missionary to Alaska, who began his ministry in Minnesota and maintained friendly ties with Westminster. Schools were as essential as churches in the West, he believed:

"I was sent to the frontier as a young missionary to do missionary work among the Indians, but as I looked over the field I could do little without the aid of a missionary teacher."

The Presbyterian Foreign Mission Board did not agree, claiming it had resources to employ only preachers. Jackson countered, "They won't come to hear preachers; send us a teacher." When the Board did not respond, Rev. Jackson began an aggressive campaign for support among Presbyterian women. He staged his own convention during the 1878 General Assembly and later organized the first national Presbyterian women's organization, the Woman's Executive Committee of Home Missions. Westminster's WHMS owed its existence to Jackson's leadership, and for decades they sent financial support to the Sheldon Jackson School at Sitka, Alaska.

\>\>\>

Ellis Island went into operation. LeElla H. Terry summarized the Westminster women's worries about immigrants who "came not to support the government but to try and overthrow it. The ranks of anarchy and socialism number no Americans—this element is entirely foreign. They boast that they can come here and cut our throats and divide our property. No wonder the church makes the immigrant population a special subject of prayer."

The women of WHMS struggled to direct their fears into positive work. Many volunteered as teachers in Westminster's own mission chapels, where first-hand experience helped to dispel prejudice. Through their work, they discovered a "genius for organization" that came as a welcome surprise. ✚

At right: Jackson is portrayed in a stained glass window on the back wall of Westminster's balcony.

A penetrating power MRS. E. F. POMEROY

"... there was no surrendering of faith or courage. When a dolorous friend spoke to her of the epithet 'widow,' she quickly replied: 'Have you forgotten the promises!'"

Westminster's energy level rose in 1880 when the Pomeroy family moved up from Cedar Rapids, Iowa. E. F. Pomeroy, a soap manufacturer, was elected to Session and went to work establishing Hope Chapel, a mission at Third Street and Ninth Avenue North. His wife, identified always as Mrs. E. F. Pomeroy, supervised its Saturday industrial school. They lost their eldest daughter, Mary, in 1881, and Mr. Pomeroy succumbed in 1883. Mrs. Pomeroy was left with four children and "very slender means," but, her friend Emma Hurd Paige remembered, "there was no surrendering of faith or courage. When a dolorous friend spoke to her of the epithet 'widow,' she quickly replied: 'Have you forgotten the promises!'"

Born Jane Carpenter in Massachusetts in 1838, Mrs. Pomeroy graduated from Mt. Holyoke Female Seminary in 1858, a rare achievement for a woman of her day. The other six of the Seven Sisters colleges did not yet exist, and only Oberlin and Antioch Colleges admitted women.

Mrs. Pomeroy organized Westminster's Woman's Home Missionary Society in 1882 and served as its president. Three years later she convinced the women of the Presbytery and Synod to take up national mission work, and she presided over the Synod Home Missionary Society for twenty years. Her leadership in the Midwest got her elected vice president of General Assembly's Woman's Board of Home Missions. Somehow she found time to head the primary department of Westminster's Sunday school for twenty-five years.

Widowhood was not her final adversity. She was disabled in an accident at sixty-five, and the next year her house burned down. Yet she lived a full life until October 27, 1918, three days after her eightieth birthday. Her obituary in Volume I of the *Westminster News* reads, "We remember that she presided with dignity and poise, that she was gifted in speech, and prayer, and her voice had a penetrating power that reached all ears." ✢

The Session minutes of March 1, 1888, record that "Wo Que, a Chinaman, a member of First Presbyterian Church of Los Angeles, California," was received into membership at Westminster. Wo had begun English lessons at the church in 1883, one of six men taught by six single women supervised by Elder J. Hyde Monroe. Some of the Chinese men had attended Presbyterian mission schools in Guangdong (Canton) province. The next to join the church, Woo Ye Sing and Wong Gee, became active, lifelong members.

About one hundred Chinese, all adult men, had come to Minnesota by 1885. The 1882 Exclusion Acts, which regarded Chinese as unassimilable aliens threatening American livelihoods, denied them citizenship and limited immigration to select merchants and teachers. The Page Law of 1875 burdened Chinese women with suspicion of "immoral purpose," due to a sexual slave trade that preyed on them. Woo Ye Sing married Liang May Seen, a victim of the slave trade who sought refuge at San Francisco's Presbyterian Mission Home in 1889, and brought her home to Minneapolis. By 1910 only nine Chinese women lived in Minnesota.

Below: A gathering of members and teachers of the Chinese Sunday School in 1948. Seven of the women pictured came to the U.S. as war brides.

At right: A hymnal used in the Chinese Sunday School in the first half of the twentieth century.

Westminster's Chinese Mission dwindled after the turn of the century. Between 1880 and 1920 the Chinese population in the United States declined by 40 percent due to return migration. Nevertheless, there were enough young men in Minneapolis in 1918 to warrant a new afternoon Sunday school, with English classes and a Cantonese Christian Endeavor group. Edward Tom and later Henry Yep kept it going. In time children's classes, Thanksgiving dinners, a Christmas pageant, and a summer picnic were added, under the direction of the Westminster Service Guild. The Japanese occupation in 1941 put China relief programs on the agenda.

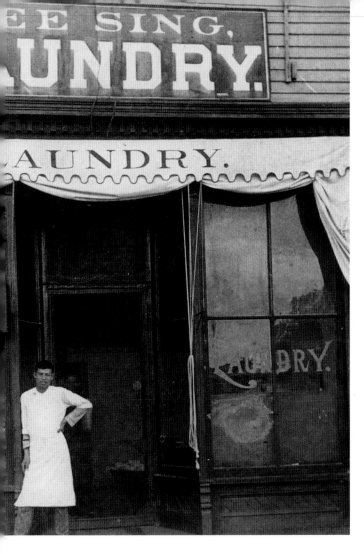

At left: Westminster member Woo Ye Sing in front of his laundry at 1319 Nicollet, 1895.

Below right: Rev. Stephen Tsui instructs two children at Saturday Chinese School.

"It provided a nice outlet for my mom," lifelong member Doris Wong says. *"I don't know that they spoke that much English. It was a way for the wives to get together. I think there was a certain amount of isolation for many of them."*

The necessity of separate programming had been questioned before the war brides arrived. Many of the longer term members attended morning worship, but those who worked late Saturday nights at restaurants preferred coming in the afternoon.

Rumors that Westminster was practicing racial segregation put an abrupt end to the Chinese Sunday school in 1957. Until the mid-1970s, there were Chinese Americans in each confirmation class. The first Chinese American officer was Roger Woo, elected to the Board of Deacons in 1969.

In 1947 the U.S. government abolished the racial restrictions in the War Brides Act passed two years before. Unmarried men set out to correct the gender imbalance in the Chinese American community. The brides brought to Westminster needed English lessons, and the babies they bore—sixteen in 1949—boosted the Sunday school population. The new superintendent, Jane Wilson, "Aunt Ayo" to the postwar generation, counted on the older women, especially Minnie Wong, Wong Gee's widow, to help the new arrivals settle in.

Westminster's intent with the Sunday school was to teach English and the Gospel, but for the participants, especially the women, it became a vital social space. The men had their business associations and Sunday games of *pai gow.* The women had Westminster.

At the urging of Chinese American members and with their financial support, the Reverend Stephen Tsui of Taiwan was called as assistant pastor from 1969 to 1975. One of his tasks was to teach the younger generation their parents' language. Between fifty and seventy-five students turned up each Saturday for Chinese School. Hopes that new immigrants would come to Westminster did not bear fruit. Most spoke Mandarin, not the Toisanese prevalent in Westminster's community, and had grown up after the Maoist revolution banned Christian missions. While fewer Chinese Americans attend Westminster than in the Sunday school's heyday, it has remained their church home for weddings and funerals. ✛

A MISSION TO THE CITY

These young women in the leg-of-mutton sleeves so stylish in the 1890s were volunteer teachers at Riverside Chapel. As such they were very likely Westminster members. Their names are lost, but readers are encouraged to look for family features.

No outreach program in Westminster's history has commanded as great a share of its time, talent, and funding as its two largest mission chapels, Hope and Riverside, both founded in 1882. Hope Chapel served North Minneapolis, first at Third Street and Ninth Avenue North, and from 1903 until 1923 at Twentieth Avenue and North Washington. Riverside began along the river in the area later known as Bohemian Flats, then moved up the bluff in three steps, settling in 1912 at the corner of Riverside and Twentieth Avenue South in the Riverside-Farrington Memorial Chapel, now the Cedar-Riverside People's Center.

The chapels' rich stories are detailed in our three previous histories in laudatory tones that suggest Hope and Riverside were anomalous Wonders of the Christian World. In fact they were examples, stellar ones, of a mission activity pioneered by the Reverend Dwight L. Moody in Chicago that engaged other churches across the country. Still, the record is impressive. The programs offered and the volunteer work that sustained them ranged wide and deep: Weekly worship services, Sabbath schools, prayer meetings, and Christian Endeavor groups. Daily kindergartens sponsored by our Woman's City Mission Society until 1921, when the public schools added kindergarten. Saturday industrial schools that taught handicrafts and self-sufficiency. Clothing distribution and health and dental clinics. Clubs for girls, boys, mothers, and young working women. Scout troops. Patriotic programs by the Daughters of the American Revolution. Lectures and stereopticon shows. Music classes and choirs. Athletic teams that brought home city championship trophies. Summer camps at Westminster's Phelps Island camp on Lake Minnetonka. Hope Chapel housed a library, and Riverside held lutefisk suppers. "No form of character-building pleasure has been frowned upon," the Reverend John Bushnell wrote in his history. But when a roller-skating rink moved in next door to Hope Chapel, Westminster threatened legal action. >>>

Next page:

"Fitch" Pabody began a diary at age ten in 1882 to improve his penmanship. He kept a close watch on Westminster. His father, a druggist, collected pew rentals at his store and served Riverside Chapel from 1890-1903, first as lay minister and then as ordained pastor.

Far right: Picnickers with tickets like this one took the streetcar and then an excursion boat across Lake Minnetonka to Westminster's camp on Phelps Island.

Near right: A brochure describing Riverside Chapel's Young Ladies Sunday School Class.

GOING

Riverside S. S. Picnic

EXCELSIOR, MINN.

August 20, 1902

Train leaves Minneapolis
St. Louis Depot, Washington
and Fourth Ave. N., at 9:30
A. M.

RETURNING

Riverside Sunday School Picnic

EXCELSIOR, MINN.

Wednesday, August 20, 1902

......ISSUED TO......

MEMBER OF PRIMARY DEPARTMENT

NOT TRANSFERABLE

Not Good for person over 8 Years Old

Train Leaves Excelsior at 4:49 P. M.

Sunday January 23, 1887
"Rev. Nathaniel West preached a good sermon this morn which
we all heard except Aunt Myra who is still troubled by her
cold. Papa went down to Hope Mission this afternoon and
reported a large thriving Sunday School. Papa and Aunt
Sara were the only ones at church there eve. It was quite
warm in the middle of the day for the snow melted slightly."

Ezra Fitch Pabody, Jr., in his diary

>>>

Westminster's lively commitment to its mission chapels was inspired by winds of change blowing in from four directions. First was a revival movement that emphasized Christ's social gospel and called for personal acts of charity toward the poor. Westminster had previously started mission chapels to plant new churches, but Hope and Riverside posed extra challenges. Their constituents' spiritual hunger could hardly be filled without attention to practical needs. Westminster volunteers could do Christ's work in as intimate a fashion as they wished, visiting the sick, teaching sewing or dental hygiene, even arranging funerals.

The second change was the revelation of urban poverty as the gritty underside of industrial progress. Even before New York photographer Jacob Riis published his eye-opening book, *How the Other Half Lives,* in 1890, Westminster members who spent time in the chapel neighborhoods knew that Minneapolis' boomtown status

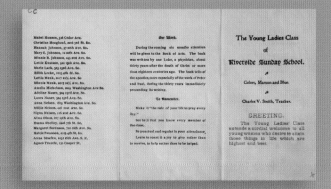

hadn't made everyone rich. Although their impulses were more charitable than reformist, they responded as citizens as well as Christians with philanthropy, evangelism, and promotion of Anglo-American values.

A third wind of change was the academic discipline of sociology, which laid the theoretical foundation for the settlement house movement of the 1890s. This new science sought to show that the social and economic conditions of people's lives determined their characters and behavior, rather than vice versa. Early intervention to relieve the effects of poverty could transform lives. When the Woman's City Missionary Society became the Kindergarten and Industrial Society, the women homed their mission on saving poor children. The Session refined its primary purpose for the chapels, declaring it to be the religious and moral education of children.

Finally, the temperance movement blew a steady breeze over the chapels' mission. The two breweries that loomed above Bohemian Flats supplied balm for disappointed hopes and the pains of hard labor. Those involved in the chapels' work saw how alcohol ravaged families. They were hardly alone in fighting demon rum. The Scandinavian American community was well populated with temperance lodges, and the leading Swedish-language newspaper, *Svenska-Amerikanska Posten,* was dedicated to temperance. The Women's Christian Temperance Union and the Anti-Saloon League also made their presence known. >>>

While the recipients of Westminster's beneficence claimed ownership of their favorite programs, Session made several attempts, often instigated by Elder James Paige, to get a firmer grip on the chapels' activities. In 1899 they took control of all chapel spending. The Session minutes include itemized bills that make a lesson in micromanagement. In 1902 the Kindergarten and Industrial Society agreed to Session's request that charity be reserved for families who attend religious services and that no child be admitted to kindergarten who was not also attending Sunday school. The kindergartens were originally open to everyone. "The children of Catholics are not debarred from these schools, and there are many who are brought in," an early announcement reads. The change may have been prompted by the arrival of Russian Jews in the Hope Chapel neighborhood, a reason for its relocation in 1903.

The people attending chapel services were to have the advantages of a church home but no expectation of independence and self-governance. The hundreds of new members received at Hope and Riverside Chapels became nominal members of Westminster, but they did not participate in Presbyterian forms of governance. This plan did not always sit well with the pastors called to serve the chapels.

Hope Chapel closed in 1923. "The coming of numbers of Catholic families, of businesses and warehouses, made it seem wise to discontinue the work," its minister, the Reverend John Connell, explained. The site where it stood is now on a slope of Interstate 94. Riverside Chapel continued to grow, until it had the largest communicants' class of any Presbyterian church in the city. It won representation on Westminster's Session in 1929 when Dr. Carl Flagstad, its superintendent, became an elder. The Presbyterian Board of National Missions conducted a study of Riverside Chapel in 1933 and recommended, "There should be a certain mutuality of life and endeavor on a more democratic level than the relation of parent and dependent child which has for so long been maintained. After fifty years, Riverside Chapel is grown up." It finally became Riverside Church in 1942. As the University of Minnesota, Interstate 94, and urban renewal claimed more and more of its neighborhood, Riverside merged in 1968 with Westminster's age mate across the river, Andrew Presbyterian Church. +

At left: Riverside Chapel boys and their teacher pose on the bluff above the Flats where the first chapel building was located. The Washington Avenue Bridge, built in 1884, crosses the Mississippi in the background.

The

City

Please designate

I hereby pledge

Do you wish en

Name

Address

Subscriptio

These girls were taught baking and other domestic skills at Riverside Chapel's Saturday industrial school to help them become self-supporting. A teacher commented in 1895 that "already these girls (from the poorest homes) had imbibed the feeling that cooking and housework was not the most elevating employment."

The ethnic origins of children in the mission chapel kindergartens in 1905

Riverside Chapel	Hope Chapel
60 Swedes	47 Scandinavians
37 Norwegians	37 Germans
24 Poles	11 Americans
19 Bohemians	7 Bohemians
11 Irish	6 Russians
9 Italians	
2 Greeks	

Poverty up close SUSAN MORSE

Westminster's Sunday bulletin of January 21, 1917, celebrates Mrs. Susan K. Morse's thirty years as director of the kindergarten at Riverside Chapel. Mrs. Morse and her longtime counterpart at Hope Chapel, Mrs. Hattie Shryock, knew the people who came to the chapel as well as anyone. As hired staff supported by the Kindergarten and Industrial Society (KIS), they reported monthly on the progress of the kindergarten, with counts of pupils enrolled, pupils attending, teachers recruited, cases of diphtheria or measles, and the hundreds of doors knocked on to locate eligible children.

Both chapels conducted mothers clubs to improve parental skills. Taking nothing for granted, Mrs. Morse went door-to-door before each mothers club meeting to deliver oral invitations. Soon she was a familiar enough figure to be trusted inside their homes. The KIS women hung on Mrs. Morse's "pathetic stories." She sat at the bedside of a dying woman "who was distressing at leaving a young daughter of fifteen with no one to look after her but a drunken father." Mrs. Morse kept her promise to find the girl a safe home. Once she had to keep liquor away from a man so he could attend his wife's funeral sober. She loaned money to a woman who needed to bury her child. The loan was repaid a month later. Due to the vigilance of Mrs. Morse and Mrs. Shryock, the KIS in 1906 placed two children in orphanages, one in the state school for neglected children, and three more in the school for the feeble-minded.

Not all of Mrs. Morse's stories were heart-rending. She laughed about expecting women with no knowledge of parliamentary procedure to conduct a meeting, and she was gratified when a mother asked for a book to help tell the Christmas story to her children.

The Sunday bulletin claims that more than three thousand kindergartners came into Mrs. Morse's hands during her tenure at Riverside Chapel. Another source says four thousand. No matter the numbers, she was a trusted advocate for residents of the neighborhood. ✚

ings and Subscriptions To-day

BE OUR ANNUAL OFFERING FOR

Mission Work.

scription (payable before next April) as indicated below.

Will Pay

s for periodical payments?

ayable to Chas. H. Curtis, Treas. of Benevolences.

Who is my neighbor? SCANDINAVIAN IMMIGRANTS

Sweden's temperance movement was a springboard for major democratic social reforms. Immigrants who had learned to claim rights of citizenship at temperance lodges back home were quick to establish lodges here. They found common cause with Presbyterians and others in countering alcohol's toll on family and civic life.

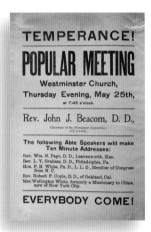

TEMPERANCE!
POPULAR MEETING
Westminster Church,
Thursday Evening, May 25th,
at 7:45 o'clock.

Rev. John J. Beacom, D. D.,
Chairman of the Permanent Committee,
will preside.

The following Able Speakers will make
Ten Minute Addresses:

Rev. Wm. N. Page, D. D., Leavenworth, Kan.
Rev. L. Y. Graham, D. D., Philadelphia, Pa.
Hon. P. H. White, Ph. D., L. L. D., Member of Congress
from N. C.
Rev. Robert F. Coyle, D. D., of Oakland, Cal.
Mrs. Wellington White, formerly a Missionary to China,
now of New York City.

EVERYBODY COME!

A 1917 Sunday bulletin relates that when Westminster undertook to serve the local poor in the 1880s, "the most needy district in the city was selected, a neighborhood unsafe for man at night or woman unattended even by day, the 'Bloody Sixth' ward, flanked by a notorious district and the 'Hub of Hell.' It was a community filled with saloons, pool-rooms, dance-halls and every conceivable evil." Bounded by the Mississippi, Franklin Avenue, and Cedar Avenue or "Snoose Boulevard," it was also teeming with Scandinavians, primarily Swedes.

Minnesota was already the New Scandinavia. Norwegians and Danes had claimed land across southern Minnesota Territory in the 1850s, and Swedes had settled Chisago and Isanti Counties. The new urban immigrants as a group were younger, less married, more female. Many had left depressed rural areas for industrializing cities in their home countries. Lured to Minneapolis by ads for laborers, they found work in lumber, flour, and woolen mills and domestic service. The maid standing by with the first course while a Westminster trustee said grace over his family's meal was, if not Irish, likely Scandinavian.

Before 1886 Westminster's rolls listed only one Scandinavian name, Peter Blomberg. Mr. and Mrs. C. C. Christianson joined the church that July, and he became the missionary at Riverside Chapel, conducting a weekly Scandinavian service. The next February Riverside received its first new member class: Charles and Sophie Anna Lindquist, Albin and Vendela Danielson, Mrs. Johanna C. Swenson, Peter and Johanna Froiseth, and Miss Carrie Morton. All lived on the Flats along the river.

Only the Lindquists made their way to Westminster itself. Chapel members were not expected to attend the mother church, but neither were they to become self-governing. In 1890 Christianson and some of his flock organized First Swedish Presbyterian Church in Cedar-Riverside, but it was short-lived, as was the Swedish Emanuel Presbyterian Church, a Synod project in the Camden neighborhood near the lumberyards upriver.

Immigrants, a 1930 wood relief by Swedish American artist Peter Wedin, portrays Swedes on their journey to America in the nineteenth century.

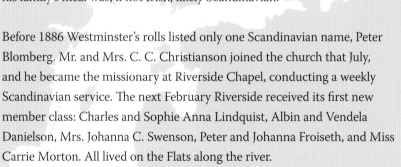

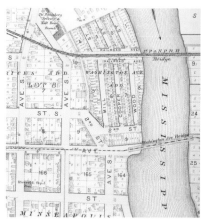

Bohemian Flats, 1898. These homes, built of driftwood from the sawmills upriver, housed Scandinavian immigrants and then the Slovaks for whom the area was named. Nearly all the houses were razed in the 1930s to make way for a barge terminal. The area is called Washington Avenue Addition in this 1892 city atlas.

Evangelizing among Lutherans in a multi-faceted immigrant community may seem frivolous, but they were not unreceptive to American Protestantism. Some, alienated by the aristocratic rigidity of Sweden's state church, had already joined pietistic movements like the Mission Covenant and Evangelical Free Churches. An 1893 map of the Elliot Park neighborhood shows ten Scandinavian churches of seven denominations. There were few churches east of Cedar Avenue where, Westminster's Kindergarten and Industrial Society reported, "Six homes out of ten bear the curse of rum."

Low wages and alcohol cast these neighbors as "others" in the eyes of the Westminster women who conducted a kindergarten, mothers club, and Saturday morning industrial school at Riverside Chapel. The women worked hard to Americanize the children and through them, their parents. After a Christmas party, one "kindergartner," as the KIS women called themselves, remarked on how the mothers had changed since she first met them: "Then they wore old shawls tied over their heads and were generally untidy." Now they were almost indistinguishable from the Westminster women, an improvement she attributed to "the refining effects of the visits of our kindergartners." In a singular accommodation to immigrant culture, KIS called the manual training class for boys the "sloyd" class, from Swedish *slöjd*, craft. A movement begun in Sweden to preserve traditional handicrafts from industrialization had caught someone's attention.

Only in subsequent generations did assimilated, upwardly mobile Scandinavian Americans slide into Westminster's pews and get elected to its boards. Arthur Sund Nelson, born to Swedish-speaking parents, became Clerk of Session in 1981. Danish ancestry proved no barrier to calling the Reverend Timothy Hart-Andersen as Pastor. And Nordic folks in the congregation take comfort in Associate Pastor Byron Thompson's Norwegian-Swedish Lutheran upbringing on Macalester Sunday, when bagpipes proclaim Westminster's Scottish dominance. ✛

A CORDIAL WELCOME TO EVERYONE.

NOT BY BREAD ALONE?

The kindergarten class at Riverside Chapel's penultimate building on the corner of Twentieth Avenue South and Two-and-a-Half Street. The University of Minnesota's West Bank campus now covers this site.

Every Saturday morning from September through March beginning in 1888, girls living near Hope or Riverside Chapel gathered at the chapel's industrial school for sewing classes. The eight-year-olds sewed on cardboard. The teenagers made their own patterns. Each paid a penny for her daily tuition so she would learn responsibility. In the afternoon the boys turned up to practice woodworking and other manual skills. Their teachers were young adults from Westminster and any friends they could recruit, plus, as the years went on, industrial school alumni. In winter a horse-drawn omnibus picked the teachers up at Westminster and delivered them to the chapels. Their work was sponsored and supervised by Westminster's Kindergarten and Industrial Society.

The last Saturday in March an end-of-the-school-year ceremony offered certificates and celebration followed by cake and ice cream. At the April 1906 KIS meeting, some sagacious guiding light questioned the "wisdom or necessity" of serving cake and ice cream to poor children whose families might not nourish them properly.

After a month's deliberation the KIS voted to discontinue the cake and ice cream in favor of something healthier. The teachers were notified in advance of the next closing ceremony.

The Riverside teachers dug into their pockets and purses and bought the cake and ice cream themselves. The teachers at Hope Chapel started an ice cream campaign and solicited enough contributions not only to furnish the treats but to buy a used piano! ✛

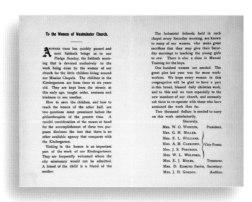

A flyer circulated by Westminster's Kindergarten and Industrial Society to encourage generous contributions on the Sunday when benevolence giving was dedicated to its city mission programs.

The Gospel at work

THE REVEREND WILLIAM E. PAUL

"You don't win people to Christ by arguing with them," Paul explained. "You win them by love and understanding."

Christ's love for "the last, the least, and the lost" guided the ministry of the Reverend William E. Paul, called as pastor of Riverside Chapel in 1907. Newly graduated from the Chicago Theological Seminary where his mentor was the Reverend Graham Taylor, a leader of the settlement house movement, Paul had also attended Taylor's Institute for Civics and Philanthropy, the country's first school for social workers. His classes brought him face-to-face with juvenile offenders, poorhouse residents, and asylum patients.

Dr. Paul's approach to ministry was four-fold: physical, mental, moral, and spiritual. Arguing that a strong, disciplined body can better withstand temptation, he persuaded Westminster to include a gymnasium and swimming pool in the new Riverside-Farrington Memorial Chapel. Athletic teams and summer camps proved more appealing to boys than manual training classes, and Faith Chapel, an outreach effort on the Flats where Riverside began, drew more Slovak participants. Paul's refusal to charge for funerals won adherents who asked him to consecrate relatives long buried in Laymen's Cemetery at Cedar Avenue and Lake Street.

In 1919 Dr. Paul was called to direct the Union City Mission, founded in 1895 as a joint response of thirteen congregations to J. Wilbur Chapman's evangelistic campaigns. Located at Hennepin and Washington in the Gateway District, it housed and fed hundreds of itinerant laborers who came to the city after the harvest to seek winter jobs in the lumber industry. Paul was still fairly new at his post when a major recession left farmers landless and farm hands unemployed. The depletion of the white pine forest reduced the need for lumberjacks and sawmill workers. Soon the Gateway became Skid Row. Where others saw bums, Dr. Paul saw trustworthy men out of work. "We believe that work is a blessing, in fact the great blessing," he said of Union City's philosophy. In 1928 he acquired land along Medicine Lake for a farm where six hundred otherwise homeless men would grow and process food, including meat, for the several thousand people per day that Union City Mission fed during the Depression. They also built and maintained a conference center that helped to fund the Mission. The infirm found respite and medical care at Mission Farm, and Minnesota's first twelve-step alcoholism treatment program opened there in 1948. The Mission's service was direct, practical, and respectful. "You don't win people to Christ by arguing with them," Paul explained. "You win them by love and understanding."

Dr. Paul spearheaded the International Union of Gospel Missions, which held its 1923 convention at Westminster. Although his ministry was explicitly non-denominational, he kept close ties to Westminster, and his family is still active in the church. After his death in 1955 his son and daughter-in-law, Horace J. (Jerry) and Phyllis Paul, served the Mission Farm until Jerry retired as superintendent. They were happy to see their home become a shelter for battered women and their children. ✛

A FERVENT PEOPLE

"Preaching will fail, singing will fail; the only thing that won't fail is a soul on fire for the concern of other souls. It is not enough for us to pray; do something."

Evangelist J. Wilbur Chapman

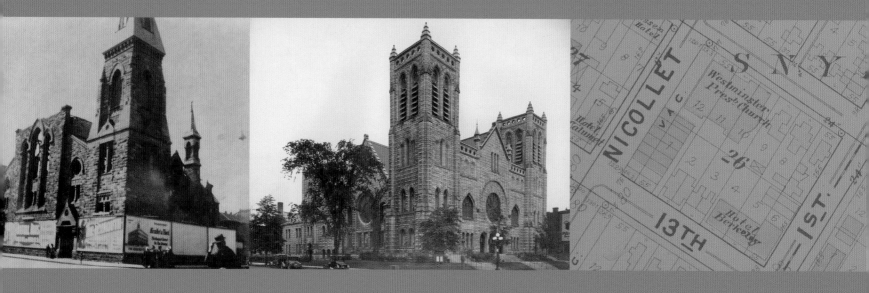

Left to right : The burned-out Seventh Street church enclosed in advertising billboards.

The Twelfth Street building, ca. 1905.

A Minneapolis atlas showing the footprint of the Twelfth Street church in 1903.

The evangelical turn

THE REVEREND DAVID JAMES BURRELL

Rev. David James Burrell (1887-91) injected Westminster with a fervently evangelical style.

After Robert Sample's long tenure, the Reverend David James Burrell brought an energetic vision for evangelism that was to guide Westminster into the twentieth century. He served as pastor for less than four years, but his passion for city missions continued long after his departure. His challenge, one member said, was to "build up a strong congregation in an old fashioned, sleepy downtown church." With a firm emphasis on four key teachings—the Bible, the cross, conversion, and activism—Westminster had always been evangelical. Burrell injected it with new style.

Out went the podium and the ministerial robes. Burrell wandered across the platform while preaching, dressed in street clothes and speaking without notes. He soon gained a city-wide reputation for eloquent, charismatic, and fearless sermons with a special appeal to the "unchurched." Church attendance increased dramatically, with between 2,000 and 2,500 attending the two Sunday services in an auditorium that seated 1,200. In just three years 713 new members joined, 345 by confession of faith.

Burrell's strong opinions drew praise and ire. One *Tribune* reporter labeled him "one of the best and most energetic of politicians" in the city, who spoke "fearlessly and effectively, against political chicanery and municipal abuses . . . against Sunday newspapers, doubtful amusements, and intemperance." Many of his sermons were reprinted and sold at newsstands. Best known was his "Can a Good Roman Catholic be a Loyal American?" (1890) with more than ten thousand copies in circulation. Its message, startling to our twenty-first century sensibilities, was a condemnation of Roman Catholic attempts to influence public education in the United States. The Roman Catholic Church was a foreign institution, Burrell charged, and it threatened the nation's republican tradition and commitment to separation of church and state.

His insistence that Westminster remain a downtown church also irritated some members. Most congregations were moving south of Eighth Street as Nicollet turned commercial. Worshipers found fewer and fewer spaces to park their buggies and sleighs. Yet Burrell contended the church must minister to the needs of the city. City mission work flourished under his direction. He spearheaded the effort to build a new chapel at Riverside for its exploding programs, and his constant promotion of mission benevolence resulted in unprecedented levels of giving: $22,300 in 1888 and $29,380 in 1889. Burrell's leadership provided a firm foundation for the next three decades, and his successors, Pleasant Hunter and John Bushnell, built on his commitments. ✦

Rev. Pleasant Hunter, who served as Westminster's pastor from 1892-1900, was on vacation in Kennebunkport, Maine, when the church burned. He sent this telegram the same day.

Bottom: The shell of the Seventh Street church, taken the day after the fire.

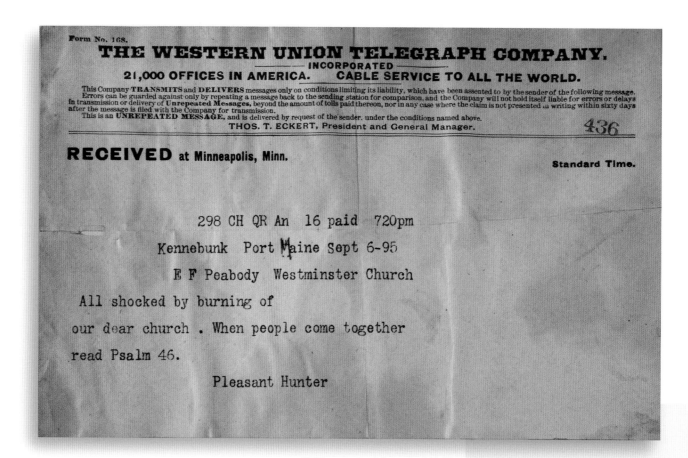

Form No. 168.

THE WESTERN UNION TELEGRAPH COMPANY.
——— INCORPORATED ———
21,000 OFFICES IN AMERICA.   CABLE SERVICE TO ALL THE WORLD.

This Company TRANSMITS and DELIVERS messages only on conditions limiting its liability, which have been assented to by the sender of the following message. Errors can be guarded against only by repeating a message back to the sending station for comparison, and the Company will not hold itself liable for errors or delays in transmission or delivery of Unrepeated Messages, beyond the amount of tolls paid thereon, nor in any case where the claim is not presented in writing within sixty days after the message is filed with the Company for transmission.
This is an UNREPEATED MESSAGE, and is delivered by request of the sender, under the conditions named above.
THOS. T. ECKERT, President and General Manager.

436

RECEIVED at Minneapolis, Minn.

Standard Time.

```
            298 CH QR An  16 paid  720pm

        Kennebunk  Port Maine Sept 6-95

            E F Peabody  Westminster Church

    All shocked by burning of

    our dear church . When people come together

    read Psalm 46.

                Pleasant Hunter
```

The west wind was brisk the night of September 5, 1895. Thunderstorms had passed through the city as Westminster members gathered at Seventh and Nicollet for their Thursday evening prayer service. After the last congregants filed out around 9:00 p.m., the janitor carefully turned off all the electrical circuits and locked the building. >>>

A FERVENT PEOPLE

>>>

A messenger boy running errands for the *Tribune* first spotted the flames at 2:00 a.m. Acting quickly, he shouted to firemen returning from another blaze. Soon flames were shooting high into the sky, threatening to engulf the church and other nearby buildings. A *Tribune* reporter described the scene: "The sight was a striking one, the lurid flames reflecting on the tall structures surrounding, and lighting up that part of the town like day. The clang of the fire gongs and the shrill whistles of the engines awakened residents of the surrounding blocks, who poured from their houses in streams." A reporter from the rival paper, the *Times*, provided more detail: "The spire of Westminster church was shown in silhouette against the bright glare of a rapidly spreading flame . . . a furnace-like flame was centered in the pinnacle over hanging the great chandelier in the center of the auditorium."

Bringing the blaze under control proved difficult. The size of the church and the location of the fire in the cupola required firemen to aim the water high. By 3:00 a.m. a portion of the roof had fallen in. Fire fighters speculated that smoldering had begun close under the roof and that the wind whipped sparks into flames and spread them throughout the building by way of the recently installed ventilation ducts.

The *Tribune* reporter later criticized the firemen for an inadequate response, but they vehemently defended their actions. More than one fire fighter was severely injured in the blaze. Fire Chief Frank Stetson had a close call. At one point he was trapped inside and escaped only by leaping through raging flames. Others reported that the building seemed charged with electricity: "I happened

to touch one of the posts and I was knocked several feet," one fire fighter explained, deepening the mystery of the fire's origins.

When dawn broke and observers got a clear look, they saw a building in ruins. The heavy Lake Superior sandstone walls still stood, but all the windows were gone. The polished black walnut interior and beautiful frescoing were destroyed. The *Tribune* reporter picked his way through the wreckage: "The pews are piled in a confusion of broken lumber and here and there among the wreckage may be seen a broken and twisted chandelier or railing. Carpets and draperies are hopelessly saturated with water which continues to flow in streams throughout the building."

Speculation about the fire's origin began immediately. One witness said the fire looked like "incendiarism," meaning arson. The *Times* suggestively called the fire mysterious: "Its origin was peculiar, not to say sensational . . . how the fire could have started in that tower at the hour is as yet an unsolved mystery." No definitive explanation ever did emerge. A city inspector confirmed that the electrical currents had been off and no fuse had been blown. The most plausible theory was that the fire had been ignited earlier in the evening by a lightning strike.

News of Westminster's disaster traveled fast. That afternoon Rev. Pleasant Hunter dashed off a telegram from his vacation retreat in Kennebunkport, Maine: "All shocked by burning of our dear church. When people come together read Psalm 46." Rev. Robert Sample telegrammed from New York City the next day and recommended Isaiah 64:1-12 and Amos 9:11. >>>

EXTRA
6 O'CLOCK.

GUTTED!

Westminster Church Is
Badly Damaged by
Fire.

Flames Destroy the Interior of the Edifice.

Origin of the Blaze Is
Something of a
Mystery.

The Loss Will Be Between $40,000 and
$50,000.

Church as theater:

The Reverend Pleasant Hunter

A large man of imposing appearance with a flair for the dramatic, the Reverend Pleasant Hunter continued the evangelical style of Dr. Burrell. With the skills of an actor, he preached with "impassioned eloquence, a flow of words like a torrent, and a heart of love." When the 1895 fire forced Westminster to stage its services in the Opera House, Hunter saw great worship possibilities in the theatrical space and advocated for similar elements in the Twelfth Street church. The new narthex resembled a theater entryway, with elegant space for conversations before and after services; the long, low podium was built like a stage and featured portable furniture. The auditorium's curvilinear pews, warm color scheme, carpeting, and visible organ pipes also contributed to the theatrical appearance. In its architectural design Westminster reflected a popular trend among wealthier evangelical congregations in the United States, to enliven church services with elements drawn from popular culture.

>>>

By 3:30 p.m. on Friday afternoon, the Trustees had gathered to review insurance policies and secure a site for Sunday services. Offers to share space had already come from nearby congregations. They eventually settled on the Grand Opera House, moving to the Lyceum Theater in November, and then to First Baptist Church at the corner of Tenth Street and Harmon Place in January 1896.

Decisions about the destroyed building were more difficult. For several years prior to the fire the Trustees had been interested in selling it and building a larger church in a more convenient location. Some considered their location too valuable for a church and detrimental to the commercial development of the city. Nearly every other congregation had relocated, but Dr. Burrell, a strong advocate for a downtown church, had opposed moving, and a slump in the real estate market kept offers low.

Months of indecision followed. Westminster's Trustees were seasoned businessmen accustomed to hard deals and setbacks. A majority had been in office when the building was first constructed in 1878-83. But the next seven months taxed their patience and tested their faith. While awaiting potential buyers, they considered rebuilding, but inspectors warned that the building was unsalvageable. They came very close to signing a purchase agreement on First Baptist Church. Two offers to buy the Seventh Street property eventually came: one from First National Bank, where former trustee Henry Sidle worked, and another from George Draper Dayton, a businessman in Worthington. Neither satisfied the Trustees, and negotiations fell through more than once. But as winter turned to spring and no other options appeared, the Trustees finally accepted Dayton's offer of two properties valued together at $50,000 and $115,000 payable in certificates of deposit. Dayton opened a dry goods store in June 1902 at Seventh and Nicollet, which he called the best piece of real estate in Minneapolis.

By late April 1896 the congregation could finally move ahead with plans for its next church home. Remarkably, new members continued to join throughout this period of uncertainty: fourteen in October, twenty-three in January, and sixteen in April. ✛

Above: The new sanctuary of the Twelfth Street church borrowed stylistic elements from the Minneapolis Opera House. This photo was taken before the organ was installed in 1898.

At right: This exterior shot of the church was taken ca. 1910.

Teacher, exemplar, and friend
THE REVEREND JOHN EDWARD BUSHNELL

At right: Outgoing and personable, Rev. John Bushnell was Westminster's longest serving pastor (1900-1930).
Below: Westminster, ca. 1910.

Westminster's longest serving pastor came almost by accident—or by providence. The pastor nominating committee found no suitable candidates after Pleasant Hunter's resignation in 1900, so they sought a supply pastor for three or four months. Their first choice turned them down; the Reverend John Edward Bushnell was second. Entirely unknown to the congregation, he arrived from New York City shortly after Christmas in 1900 and immediately made an impression. He organized a "watch night meeting" for New Year's Eve, the dawn

of the new century, with three hours of preaching, singing, and prayers. Even with only three days' notice, the congregation flocked to the meeting and instantly warmed to him. Two weeks later the Session offered him a permanent position, which extended to thirty years. His tenure spanned one of the most tumultuous periods in American religious history.

Dr. Bushnell was well equipped for the task. Outgoing and personable, with a gentle humor and a gift for words, he elicited tremendous loyalty from the congregation. Occasionally his informality provoked concern. In 1912 "a large number of the membership" requested that he wear a ministerial gown during services. Later an elder complained of his use of the American Revised Bible in the pulpit rather than the familiar King James Version. Both times Session deferred to Bushnell's judgment, and he no doubt responded with sympathy and grace. Under his leadership Westminster grew into the denomination's sixteenth largest congregation in 1925, with a membership of 2,343: 1,720 at Westminster, 470 at Riverside Chapel, and 153 at Hope Chapel.

More evangelical than intellectual, Bushnell preferred to invite representatives from the Salvation Army, Moody Bible Institute, and the Anti-Saloon League as guest speakers rather than eminent theologians. When Dr. Francis L. Patton, a professor at Princeton Theological Seminary, delivered five lectures at Westminster on "Christianity and the Modern Man," Bushnell joked that "all professed to have enjoyed" it and "some" may even have understood it. Preaching the Gospel, encouraging missions near and far, and comforting his flock in times of suffering were his talents and passions.

On his sixty-fifth birthday in 1923 special greetings were printed in the Sunday bulletin: "We . . . express our warm gratitude for the years of service in our midst. We honor him as teacher, exemplar and friend. We remember today that he preaches to us the full riches of the Gospel of Christ, ever impelling us onward to be doers and not merely hearers." ✛

KEEPING THE SABBATH HOLY

Are you a "oncer" or a "twicer"? Westminster's congregants in the early twentieth century would have known exactly what that question meant. Families could attend a Sunday morning service followed by Sunday school for all ages and return in the evening to worship again.

Observance of the Sabbath has changed dramatically over our 150-year history. Sunday in 1857 was clearly set apart for worship and quiet reflection. Many local Presbyterians no doubt followed the guidance offered by Rev. Edward D. Neill in his 1856 book, *A Handbook for the Presbyterian Church in Minnesota, Designed to Promote Order in and Love for the Sanctuary.* "It is the duty of every person to remember the Lord's Day, and to prepare for it before its approach," he wrote.

"It is requisite that there be holy resting, all the day, from unnecessary labors; and an abstaining from those recreations which may be lawful on other days; and also, as much as possible, from worldly thoughts and conversation. . . . Let the time . . . be spent in reading, meditation, repeating of sermons, catechizing, religious conversation, prayer for a blessing upon the public ordinances, the singing of psalms, hymns, or spiritual songs, visiting the sick, relieving the poor, and in performing such like duties of piety, charity, and mercy."

Concerned that breaking the Sabbath could cause irreparable harm, Rev. Robert Sample warned in an 1877 sermon, "A corruption of morals usually follows a profanation of the Sabbath." Rev. David James Burrell adamantly opposed Sunday publication of the newspaper and joined ten other local Presbyterian pastors in an 1889 entreaty to parishioners "to abstain from patronizing it as an advertising medium and from either purchasing or reading it." Westminster members, too, took part in the Friends of the Christian Sabbath, an organization that worked to protect Sunday's sanctity with the regulations we know as "blue laws."

The Sunday evening service went into steady decline and was eliminated in 1939. Rev. John Bushnell lamented in 1919, "I often wonder how it came to pass that Church members suddenly and as if in concert threw off all sense of obligation for the Sunday evening Church service, and what they are doing with the time of that service. The Pastor does not recognize more than one in ten of those present at that Sunday service. Where are the nine? Are they at home praying for the Kingdom? Are they yearning for the bringing of the world to the Saviour? Will the church save America on such a working basis as this?" What would he think about watching TV on Sunday nights?

A variety of social and cultural shifts caused the decline in Sunday observance. Suburbanization was one culprit. As congregants moved farther from the center of town, they were less likely to return for evening services. Rising prosperity was another. In 1934 evening services were suspended for the first time in summer months because so many people headed to their cottages. >>>

Above: Quiet, meditative Sunday outings were encouraged during the nineteenth century, but Sunday newspapers were considered a profanation of the Sabbath. Depicted here are members of Riverside Chapel.

At right: The Young People's Society for Christian Endeavor engaged youth in wholesome Sunday activities. This is a Fourth of July outing to Phelps Island in 1914.

A President Visits

When President William Howard Taft came to worship at Westminster on September 19, 1909, during a three-day visit to Minneapolis, there were few indications inside the church that a man of such eminence was present. While crowds thronged outside, pew holders quietly filed into their seats. The service featured no special music, no special decoration other than a small silk flag draped over a table, and no special mention of the visitor except for a petition during the congregational prayer for the president's safety. Seated in the center front pew with Dr. Cyrus Northrop, president of the University of Minnesota, President Taft "seemed especially pleased that Dr. Bushnell's sermon contained no reference to his presence," the *Journal* reported. Only one incident, during the offering, drew a comment from Taft:

"I had my money in my fingers, but no one would pass me the plate. They evidently thought I was only a poor president and needed the money."

>>>

The lure of leisure-time pursuits also exacted its toll, as Dr. Bushnell recognized: "The movies struck the church Sunday night, golf delivered its heavy blow Sunday morning, and the automobile came along to augment the secular invasion by cutting off the week-ends. Thus it cannot be disguised that every blessing extracts its toll." When the start of the worship service was moved from 11:00 a.m. to 10:30 a.m. in 1970, one explanation offered was that the change would allow worshipers to make the Vikings kick-off.

Westminster's patterns of congregational life have continued to respond to changes in Sabbath observance. As evening services declined in the 1930s, attention shifted to evening youth programs. Sunday evening remained an important fellowship time through the 1960s. A desire for alternative forms and settings for worship has recently produced the monthly Celtic services in the chapel on Thursday evenings. Although the church sits vacant many Sunday evenings, the block of time devoted to church activities on Sunday mornings has grown considerably. A parishioner may arrive for adult education or choir practice at 9:15 a.m., attend the 10:30 a.m. service, and linger over conversation and coffee in the Heller Commons until well after noon. ✝

A WESTMINSTER PIONEER OBSERVES THE SABBATH

"I often wonder how it came to pass that Church members suddenly and as if in concert threw off all sense of obligation for the Sunday evening Church service, and what they are doing with the time of that service. The Pastor does not recognize more than one in ten of those present at that Sunday service. Where are the nine? Are they at home praying for the Kingdom? Are they yearning for the bringing of the world to the Saviour? Will the church save America on such a working basis as this?" Rev. John Bushnell in 1919

Twenty-three-year-old Samuel A. Harris devoted his Sundays entirely to activities at Westminster, or at least that is what he wrote to his mother in Goshen, Indiana, on April 19, 1870: "The Sabbath comes again with its blessed rest. . . . Of course I mean rest in its truest sense, for a Sabbath truly spent is far from being idly spent. Often I think that my Sabbath day work is much more severe than my weekly work. . . . Lately it has been my prayer, as Sabbath approaches, that I may be prepared to keep it Holy unto the Lord. . . . Every time I have done this I have noticed a change, or rather a state of feeling, that I knew was impossible to be wrought by self. No matter how full of care and business I would be Saturday Evening, even if I would think I could not get this or that matter off my mind tomorrow . . . yet when Sabbath Day comes the care and business is all gone. . . . I am enabled to enjoy the services of the day and to go to my Sabbath School Class with a desire to do good, and a love for the work, and I trust with the presence of Christ with me."

Eighteen years later, after attaining the presidency of Northwestern National Bank in Minneapolis, Harris had adopted new Sabbath-keeping habits:

"Sunday at Lake Minnetonka is not an ideal Sabbath. The cottage for most part devotes the day to pleasure. Perhaps a few, such as brother CTT [Charles T. Thompson] go to the city to church, but the great majority go on the lake or stay quietly at home. For me the going to town for service does no good. I am so disturbed and secularized by the train . . . that the keen edge of the Sabbath feeling is taken off. . . . A perfect autumn Sabbath day. Spent good part of time lying in hammock. . . . It was a lazy day but I believe the good Lord intends his busy creatures should sometimes fall into such a state." ✣

Riverside Chapel picnickers.

THE RADIO AISLE AND OTHER FIRSTS

Each Sunday for many years, Don Scherbert managed the sanctuary sound system from this modest desk stationed just outside the sanctuary doors.

Long before Robert Schuller's "Hour of Power" or Krista Tippett's "Speaking of Faith," Westminster was riding the media wave. In January 1923 it became the first church in the region to broadcast its Sunday morning services on the radio. Three forward-thinking elders, Richard Tomlinson, George Murphy, and James Inglis, recognized the potential of the new technology and arranged a contract with WLAG (later WCCO) at a cost of $1,200. It was a visionary move. Only three years before, the first radio news broadcasts had begun in Detroit, Michigan. Some feared radio would put the church out of business. One local pastor even called it "an invention of the devil to keep people away from church." Dr. Bushnell believed it had the opposite effect:

> *"It was a revelation to note how many persons and families . . . are deprived of ordinary church privileges for various reasons beyond their control to whom the radio service . . . has come as an unspeakable blessing."* ✛

1889	**1894**	**1900**	**1918**	**1922**	**1923**
First telephone installed in the Seventh Street church	Ventilation system installed in the Seventh Street church	Extension telephone installed for Mr. Curtis, Assistant Pastor	Automobile purchased for Mr. Strock, Assistant Pastor, to aid with visitation. Cost: $500	Two loud speakers installed in the sanctuary for $15	Sunday morning services broadcast by WLAG
Electric lights installed					

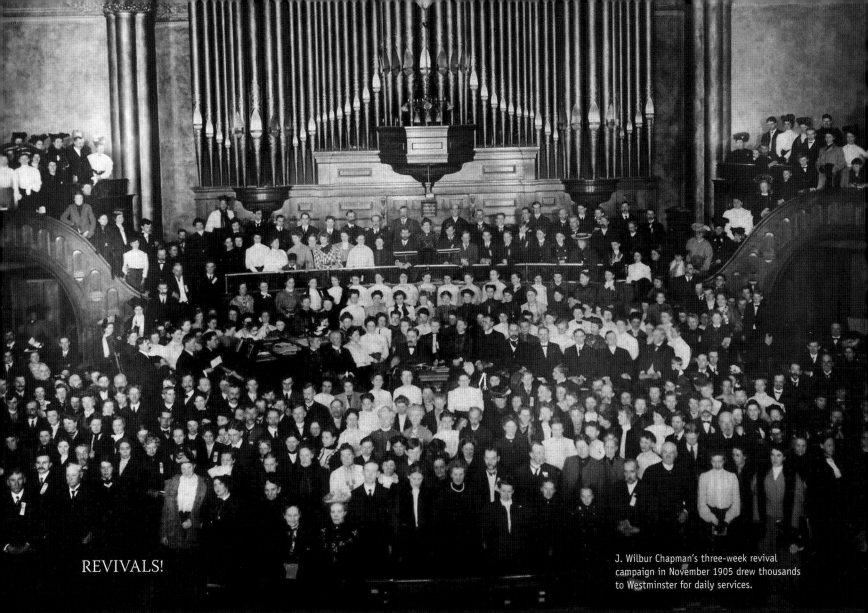

REVIVALS!

J. Wilbur Chapman's three-week revival campaign in November 1905 drew thousands to Westminster for daily services.

No *frenzy, no fanaticism, no skirmishing,"* Mark Twain wrote of his mild-mannered denomination in 1866. *"You never see any of us Presbyterians getting in a sweat about religion and trying to massacre the neighbors."* By 1900 only a portion of that statement still held true. Urban revival meetings swept across the nation in the early twentieth century with powerful orators calling sinners to repentance and renewal. Westminster fully embraced this phenomenon between the 1890s and the 1920s, as it hosted famed evangelists T. DeWitt Talmage, Reuben Torrey, W. K. Lane, Gipsy Smith, and others. The largest of Westminster's revivals occurred in November 1905 when the Reverend J. Wilbur Chapman rolled into town with his twenty-five trained assistants. It was a peak period for evangelism on both sides of the Atlantic in 1904-06. >>>

>>>

Westminster's revivals followed a more deliberate pattern. Filled with songs and prayers but marked by decency and good order, they resembled what one historian has labeled a "businessman's revival," planned to fit the lives of busy people, who might slip in a midday meeting between clients. Chapman's message to noon crowds was a constant variation on a single theme:

"A man can succeed in business and be a Christian."

J. Wilbur Chapman was both thoroughly Presbyterian and broadly ecumenical. His career as an evangelist began shortly after he became pastor of New York's prestigious Fourth Presbyterian Church in 1889, when General Assembly tapped him to lead an aggressive nationwide campaign. His style suited their needs. He was a college graduate and a man of culture, not one of the "reformed drunkard" types. Always dressed immaculately in a long black frock coat and a black Windsor tie, he appealed to the educated middle classes. Described as a "delicious mind, brain and heart stirrer," he combined dignity with verbal punch in his platform presentation.

His organizational methods were renowned. Before he came to any city, Chapman demanded evidence of interdenominational cooperation. In Minneapolis, dozens of Protestant churches joined in, but Westminster was where he chose to preach. His assistants were dispatched to Plymouth Congregational, First Baptist, Oliver Presbyterian, and many others.

The scenes at Westminster would be hard for us to recognize. With more than 2,000 attending noon meetings and more cramming in for nightly services, hundreds of ushers helped the crowds find seats. Attendance on Sundays

was boosted by a new law closing saloons on the Lord's Day. "Nearly all" of Minneapolis attended at least one gathering, the *Journal* suggested, with many returning for multiple visits. The music alone was a draw, featuring both gospel tunes and old standbys: "In the Sweet Bye and Bye," "Nearer My God to Thee," "Crown Him with Many Crowns," "All Hail the Power of Jesus' Name." Enthusiasm swelled throughout the campaign, although activity stopped briefly on Saturday, November 4, when between 28,000 and 36,000 spectators headed to Northrop Field for the fiercest football game of the season, between Minnesota and Wisconsin. (The Badgers won.)

Each day hundreds of people "came to Christ." Here, the *Journal* describes one Thursday evening service at Westminster: "'Lost Opportunities' was the subject which Dr. Chapman handles with moving power. Serious thoughts were awakened; heart strings were touched and the audience was fairly melted to tears. In the after meeting the scenes were remarkable. Persons from all walks in life came to express their new belief in Christ. Sobs broke the quiet of the hour and tears flowed freely, either of joy or of remorse from awakened consciences." All of this made for "peace, prosperity and progress," the *Journal* declared.

Membership soared in the six months following Chapman's visit. Westminster hired a temporary deaconess to help visit the people who had signed cards during the campaign, and Session held almost weekly meetings for the following three months to receive 205 new members.

Revivalism was the product of a particular moment. By the 1920s these campaigns became less frequent in mainstream churches as debates over modernism altered the religious landscape. A cautious conservatism had set in by the 1950s. When opportunities arose to participate in Billy Graham's crusades in 1959 and 1961, Westminster's Session opted out, preferring to cling to a new version of "decency" and "good order." ✦

J. Wilbur Chapman's revivals spanned the United States. This cartoon depicts a scene from his Boston campaign in January 1909.

A FERVENT PEOPLE

In 1914 Session weighed a proposal to host the controversial but enormously popular Billy Sunday, a former major-league second baseman turned evangelist. Known for his "aggressive, militant masculinity," Billy Sunday cared little for conventional religion and delighted in excoriating the "weak-kneed, thin-skinned, pliable, plastic, spineless, effeminate, ossified, three-carat Christianity" of liberal Protestants. Westminster's leaders were anxious to find ways to attract and keep men as active members, and Billy Sunday seemed to be the answer.

On average nationwide in the early twentieth century, only a third of church members were male, a pattern duplicated at Westminster both then and now. With a predominance of women in the pews, Protestant Christianity was increasingly perceived as "feminine." Women were seen as more spiritual and their loyalty to religion beyond question. By contrast, men were tagged as secular. Caught in the wheels of commerce and constantly tempted by drink and infidelity, they required special measures, above and beyond the normal ministrations of the church. Revival campaigns and special church programming aimed to win them back.

As a downtown church Westminster reached out to businessmen. The new professional man with multiple pulls on his time was replacing the old style of committed churchman exemplified by Charles Vanderburgh and C. T. Thompson. C. W. Van Tuyl, chair of Westminster's prayer meeting committee, put his finger on the problem in 1913 when he complained of men's dismal attendance at the Thursday evening prayer meetings: "We believe that the defect . . . is a failure to recognize the influence of two essential characteristics of our day, namely a more cultivated, possibly more satiated, intelligence and the far greater pressure of modern life in its demands upon the time and vital force of the kind of men who constitute the greater part of our . . . city congregations. These men are very busy . . . their days and their evenings are crowded full. . . . Many people feel that they simply cannot spare the time."

Awakening men's desire for service was one strategy. Inspiration sprang from The Men and Religion Forward Movement (M&RFM), a nationwide religious revival which came to Westminster in October 1911. Organized by an interdenominational group of ministers including Charles Stelzle, famed proponent of the social gospel who got his start at Westminster's Hope Chapel, the M&RFM hit seventy-six major cities and more than a thousand small towns in its seven-month tour of the United States. When its executive director F. B. Smith was asked why he didn't leave church work to women, who already had a monopoly on it, he replied: "When a man is drowning, you don't send a lady out to rescue him. You send a great, big, he-man."

The M&RFM aimed at "vitalizing" churches by encouraging men to volunteer skills developed in business and politics. A spokesman told the *Minneapolis Journal*, "This movement is Christian social service, rather than evangelism. We are trying . . . to educate local workers, arouse their interest and start them along a line of activity . . . also we are trying to stimulate Bible study, work among boys, [and] community extension." "Muscular Christianity" spoke in the language of the new consumerist world. Men needed modern, manly outlets in church work. >>>

Westminster men in a tug-of-war, probably at a father-and-son event about 1930.

55

>>>

Ministry to boys also drew attention. "We as a Church are doing little for our boys. We seem lamentably behind other organizations in this regard," the Clerk of Session complained in 1915. Earlier programs such as the Boys' Brigade had declined. Attempts to draw boys in through summer programs failed miserably due to poor leadership. A more successful strategy emerged in 1918 when Westminster established one of the city's first Boy Scout troops, Troop 33. Camp Ajawah followed in the 1920s.

When men's church attendance did not immediately rise, some Westminster elders grew bolder: Billy Sunday might be the answer. Ultimately they decided against inviting him, perhaps judging his style too strong. Later, Harry Emerson Fosdick, author of the popular 1911 book *The Manhood of the Master*, spoke at Westminster. The early twentieth-century Jesus had muscles, too. ✛

Before J. Wilbur Chapman arrived in any city, he sent ahead teams of investigators to compile statistics on church-going rates. Their data for Minneapolis was printed in the *Journal* on October 3, 1911:

Number of churches: 201

27	Methodist	45	Lutheran
21	Presbyterian	9	Jewish
21	Catholic	24	Congregational
22	Baptist	15	Episcopal

Number of saloons: 418

Distribution of denominational membership (Protestants only)

18%	Methodist	16%	Presbyterian
17%	Baptist	12%	Episcopal
16%	Lutheran	1%	Unitarian

Gender ratio of church membership

65%	women
35%	men

Above: A men's retreat in November 1969. Associate Pastor Tom Zemek and Bob Olson are at the center of the photo. The balding man is likely Andy Hobart.

At right: An activity at a rainy-day church picnic in 1984 puts Gordon Hermanson, Bruce Jones, Associate Pastor Bill Rolland, and others to a test of, well, something.

A most loveable Christian gentleman CHARLES T. THOMPSON

"Generous almost to a fault, affectionate and sympathetic of heart, gracious and refined in address, he moved among us as a most loveable Christian gentleman, adorning the doctrine he professed by a life of charity and arduous endeavor."
Memorial to C. T. Thompson from Westminster's Session, December 1914.

Few have given as much to Westminster as Charles T. Thompson. Born in Glendale, Ohio, in 1853, Thompson moved to Minneapolis in 1878 and promptly joined the church. Blessed with a knack for gaining people's confidence, he was elected Clerk of Session two years later, a position he held for nearly thirty-five years.

"When I was elected clerk . . . I went straight home and got down on my knees and asked the Lord to make me the best session clerk that ever was," he later confessed. The result, one friend suggested, should be noted in some permanent record of "remarkable answers to prayers."

Nearly every aspect of Westminster's ministry bore his energetic imprint. Riverside Chapel got its start when he purchased it in 1882 for $160. Westminster's Sunday school grew under his leadership as superintendent. Area churches sought his legal and financial advice. Macalester College stabilized its budget during his fourteen years of service on its board. General Assembly benefited from his service on dozens of committees, including one to revise the Westminster Confession in 1901. Thompson was widely recognized as an authority on Presbyterian law, procedure, and history, and hailed as "one of the best known elders of the denomination." In 1910 he was elected Vice Moderator of General Assembly, the highest lay position in the Presbyterian Church. He also authored, with efficiency and flair, the first book-length history of Westminster, published in time for the church's fiftieth anniversary in 1907.

So devoted was Thompson to Westminster that he never bought a house in town, preferring to rent lodgings as close to the church as possible. In the summer his wife, Kate, and their three sons retreated to a cottage on Lafayette Bay in Minnetonka, next-door to his brother-in-law Samuel Harris. But Thompson made the daily commute into town for his thriving law practice and church meetings.

When he died unexpectedly in November 1914, allegedly of food poisoning, Thompson left Westminster its first permanent endowment. His will designated that the proceeds from a $5,000 principal (more than $100,000 in 2007 values) be divided among Presbyterian church boards and Westminster's city missions.

"He was a man of Abrahamic faith," Judge Ell Torrance remarked at Thompson's memorial service at Macalester in December 1914. "He believed in the divinely appointed agency of the Church—not one branch only but all branches of the Church having a vital connection with Jesus Christ."

Thompson's spirit lives on today. On some quiet days at the church, retired Facilities Manager Al Cooper confides, one can still smell the smoke from Thompson's omnipresent pipe. ✛

Stained-glass Christ window in the narthex given by Samuel Harris, Thompson's brother-in-law.

YOUTH MINISTRY

The Young People's Society for Christian Endeavor (YPSCE), a worldwide organization with a thriving branch at Westminster in the early twentieth century, invented the concept of youth ministry. This event is in Glenwood Park, now Wirth Park, in 1913.

"Hallowe'en revels, skating parties, musicales, picnics, corn-roasts . . . . We know how to be gay without being giddy and can be happy without being hilarious."

Inspiring young people to lives of Christian service has been a steady priority for Westminster. In 1858 its founders established a Sabbath school to introduce children to the Christian faith. Later the "discovery" of adolescence focused attention on the crucial teenage years. By the 1900s a kaleidoscope of organizations offered young people at Westminster and its missions opportunities for fellowship, education, and spiritual growth: the Cheerful Givers, Hope Reapers, Pearl Gatherers, Gleaners, Daughters of the King, Band of Hope, Seek and Save Band, Little Girls' Praying Band, and the Boys' Missionary Brigade were but a few.

None was quite so enthusiastic as the Young People's Society for Christian Endeavor (YPSCE), credited with inventing the concept of youth ministry. Launched in 1881 by Dr. Francis E. Clark, a Congregationalist minister in Portland, Maine, Christian Endeavor quickly spread across the globe, with sixty-seven thousand youth-led branches and four million members by 1906. A branch of YPSCE came to Westminster in 1888 under the sponsorship of Rev. David James Burrell. Nearly a hundred young men and women immediately joined. Branches also opened at the mission chapels and later in Westminster's Chinese community.

The key to Christian Endeavor's success was an emphasis on unfettered leadership. Young people took charge of their own programs. They staged Sunday evening services that drew upwards of one hundred, volunteered at the Petran and Union City Missions in the Gateway district, organized variety shows for Hopewell Hospital, and raised hundreds of dollars for mission projects. When half their membership volunteered for service in World War I, those at home organized weekly letter-writing circles. It was not all work, though, as Jennie Congdon testified: "Hallowe'en revels, skating parties, musicales, picnics, corn-roasts . . . . We know how to be gay without being giddy and can be happy without being hilarious."

Christian Endeavor shared its optimism with other international youth organizations. The British-based Student Christian Movement proudly proclaimed the slogan, "The Evangelization of the World in this Generation." By 1918 the slogan had disappeared. Westminster's YPSCE declined after the war and folded in 1925, a casualty of postwar pessimism. ✦

ABBOTT HOSPITAL

When Westminster's Board of Trustees inherited Dr. Amos W. Abbott's thirty-five-bed hospital from its benefactor, William Hood Dunwoody, in 1914, the association of religious institutions with hospitals had strong precedent. Cottage Hospital, the first in Minneapolis, was opened under the auspices of the Episcopal Church in 1870 and later renamed St. Barnabas. St. Mary's Hospital was Catholic; Deaconess was Norwegian Lutheran, and Asbury, Methodist. A hospital owned by a single congregation was, however, unusual.

Even with a hired administrator and full staff, the hospital and nursing school drew countless volunteer hours from Westminster. If the Trustees wrote Abbott's history, the text would be weighted with legal jargon and six- and seven-digit financial figures. If it were left to the Auxiliary, founded in 1929, poignant stories, profiles of patients and medical personnel, and fundraising for amenities and for support of student nurses would predominate. The clergy could tell of bedside visits and of Bible classes and baccalaureate services for the student nurses. A more intimate measure of Abbott's >>>

Counter-clockwise from top:

Dr. Amos Wilson Abbott.

Operating Room Number One, 1920.

The Reverend Henry Chace, an assistant and associate pastor at Westminster from 1950-69, was a frequent and welcome visitor at the bedsides of Abbott patients.

Children in the hospital's Janney Pavilion, funded by Westminster Trustee Thomas B. Janney and his wife, Mary.

The Janney Pavilion, built in 1921, was a precursor of Minneapolis Children's Hospital.

value would come from the many Westminster members who chose, and still choose, to trust their medical care to the church's own hospital.

Abbott re-organized as a non-profit corporation in 1963, with Westminster members on its board, then merged in 1970 with Northwestern Hospital, founded in 1882 as a charity hospital for women and children. Church officer and attorney John Holten can best recount that phase of Abbott's history.

Abbott vacated its site on First Avenue South at Seventeenth Street in 1980 and moved all facilities to the enlarged Northwestern campus at Twenty-sixth Street and Chicago Avenue South. Westminster's attention has returned to the old block: The Abbott View apartments across Eighteenth Street from the old hospital building are the first achievement in a joint affordable housing initiative with Plymouth Congregational Church and Plymouth Church Neighborhood Foundation established in 2006.

Allina, the health network that runs Abbott-Northwestern Hospital, relates the history of the hospital on its website. It makes no mention of Westminster. ✚

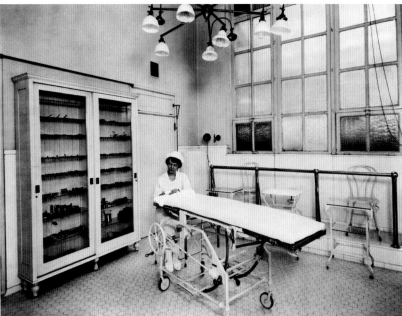

WESTMINSTER'S FIRST FEMALE ASSISTANT PASTOR?

Long before women could be ordained as ministers, they exercised their pastoral talents in unofficial ways. A non-ordained woman could indeed be counted as Westminster's first female assistant pastor.

As Westminster grew in size and complexity, Session deemed it necessary to hire additional staff. The Reverend Charles H. Curtis arrived in 1897 as the first ordained pastoral assistant to support Pleasant Hunter in his mounting tasks. He was followed by a series of young assistant ministers, none of whom stayed very long. As transitions occurred, Session relied on creative staffing solutions. For instance, in late 1913 the pastor's assistant, the Reverend James Melrose, fell gravely ill, and his doctors forbade "mental work for a year." With no disability insurance Melrose and his family looked to the church for support. Session voted to continue his salary for six months and searched for a cheap replacement.

Miss Ida L. Seymour was the solution. A member of Marble Collegiate Church in New York City, she came with effusive recommendations from Rev. David James Burrell, Westminster's pastor in the early 1890s. A young, single career woman, she worked in a "very responsible position in a New York importing house," but longed to enter religious work "even at a much lower salary." Session hired her as a deaconess to aid with visitation and outreach. She made more than two thousand visits each year to the homes of Westminster members. Miss Seymour had no formal training, but she proved so effective that her title quickly became Assistant to the Pastor. Known for her "gracious way of delivering prayers and devotionals," she unofficially filled the role of assistant pastor until the church hired Melrose's replacement four years later.

Seymour of course stayed on in her designated job. Her salary was one thousand dollars per year, one quarter of what the church paid Mr. Melrose and just a little more than the janitor's salary at Riverside Chapel. She served Westminster with aplomb until her death in 1934. ✛

1832	1848	1888	1906	1912
General Assembly (GA) forbids women "to teach and exhort, or to lead in prayer, in public and promiscuous assemblies."	Elizabeth Cady Stanton, a Presbyterian, helps organize the Seneca Falls Convention on women's rights	Louisa Woosley is first woman licensed to preach in Cumberland branch of Presbyterian Church	GA approves female deacons in the PCUSA	Women allowed to speak at GA for the first time—about the Women's Board of Home Missions

HOPE IN HARD TIMES

*God is not an earthquake, a whirlwind.
God is in the still, small voice unheeded
by the passing throng.*

Dr. William H. Boddy, "Light in Days of Discouragement," sermon preached at Westminster on
October 16, 1938, just days after the Munich Conference, at which Neville Chamberlain "appeased"
Hitler by sacrificing Czechoslovakia

Men at the Union City Mission, 1925.

A regular monthly newsletter to Westminster members began during World War I to convey news of members serving in the war.

When news arrived in March 1918 of Edwin C. Phinney's death in a YMCA hospital in France, shock and sadness settled over the congregation. This popular thirty-six-year-old deacon was Westminster's first casualty in World War I, and his death shattered the illusion that this community was exempt from wartime suffering. The Session felt moved to compose a statement of their unwavering faith:

> *"Now therefore be it resolved, THAT the membership of Westminster Church, while seeking to bow to the will of God, recognizes that in the death of Edwin C. Phinney, the church, the community, and the cause of humanity for which he gave his life have suffered an irreparable loss: THAT, impelled by this first golden star to appear on our service flag, we strive for a higher degree of patriotism and a greater determination to 'carry on' until Kaiserism shall have met its certain doom."*

Since August 1914 war had raged in Europe over confusing causes and murky aims. Casualties among the French, Belgians, British, and Germans reached the millions, as new technologies like mustard gas and machine guns outpaced military strategy. Through the first three grueling years of war, the United States hung back, unwilling to get embroiled in the distant conflict.

Many interpreted the war as an apocalyptic event, the result of decadent European traditions. "The wages of sin is death," wrote one Texas congressman in a popularly held opinion. "The nations, now drunk on blood, rioting in ruinous war, are paying the death penalty because their sins have found them out. Given over to ravenous greed, with a riotous aristocracy living in luxury and lust, ruling in rapacity . . . they are now reaping the harvest of their sowing."

The United States stood righteously apart from the chaos. When the youth group Daughters of the King opened their meetings with the song "America the Hope of the Nations," they expressed a deeply held belief in America's ordained role.   >>>

Humor on the Battlefield

After the offensive at Château-Thierry, Champagne, in July 1918, Westminster member James Thompson found aid in an unexpected place: "Right now I am wearing brand new underwear 'made in Germany.' One of the fellows and I found a sack of it abandoned by some Boche leaving in a hurry. The shirts came below my knees and by cutting slits in the top of pants I can use them as union suits. They were evidently made for the 1913 Hun model."

June 1914	August 1914	July 1915
Archduke Franz Ferdinand and his wife are assassinated by a Serbian nationalist in Sarajevo	War officially begins when Germany declares war on Russia and France	128 American lives lost when a German U-Boat sinks the British liner Lusitania

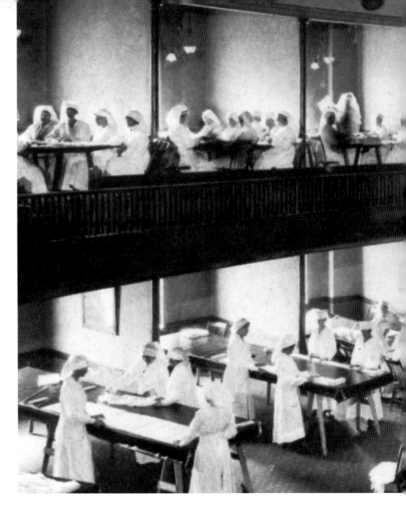

At right: Westminster's Red Cross unit, working here in Westminster's pre-renovation assembly hall and Sunday school rooms, was one of the region's largest.

>>>

Westminster paid little heed to the conflict at first. In August 1914 the Session was considering complaints of inadequate toilet facilities in the building. Congregants gathered at a few hastily organized prayer meetings but otherwise went about their daily lives. As hostilities dragged into a second year, voluntarism replaced apathy. Sympathy for Belgian women and children violated by the German "menace" spurred unprecedented rates of civilian mobilization. In 1915 the pastor's wife, Mrs. J. E. Bushnell, and Mrs. C. E. Rittenhouse organized a Red Cross unit at Westminster, which by some accounts became the largest station in the Northwest. Between 200 and 250 volunteers gathered several days a week to sew clothes, knit socks and sweaters, prepare surgical dressings, and roll on average 5,000 gauze bandages a month. Conversations flowed across worktables and continued over the daily lunches and Thursday suppers for the volunteers. Through the McCall Mission in France, Westminster women "adopted" (sent aid to) five war orphans, French and Belgian children who had lost fathers in the conflict. More aid went to Armenian orphans and refugees.

Westminster's men also contributed to the civilian war effort. Elder E. J. Couper took charge of raising nearly fifty thousand dollars for the YMCA Western Division and later served on the National Commission of War Work in Europe. Trustee James Ford Bell chaired a national committee to organize the flour industry. Frank T. Heffelfinger managed the Red Cross Northwestern Division. Dr. Bushnell served several stints as a chaplain at Camp Dodge in Iowa.

Once the United States entered the conflict in April 1917, the church's young people paid the highest price. Altogether, 178 men and 13 women from Westminster served in Europe. The best educated and most prosperous were among the first to enlist. One record indicates that half the Christian Endeavor membership volunteered for service. Seven would never come home. One of them was Private Fred C. Wagner of the U.S. Marines, who was killed "about July 15" in Château-Thierry near the Ardennes in northern France. He had come to Westminster from North Dakota when he entered Macalester College in preparation for Christian ministry. Those who did return bore physical and mental scars.

July 1916	November 1916	February 1917	March 1917
60,000 British soldiers lost in a single day during the Battle of the Somme	Woodrow Wilson re-elected president with the campaign slogan "He kept us out of the war"	Germany resumes unrestricted submarine warfare	President Wilson's cabinet votes unanimously to declare war on Germany

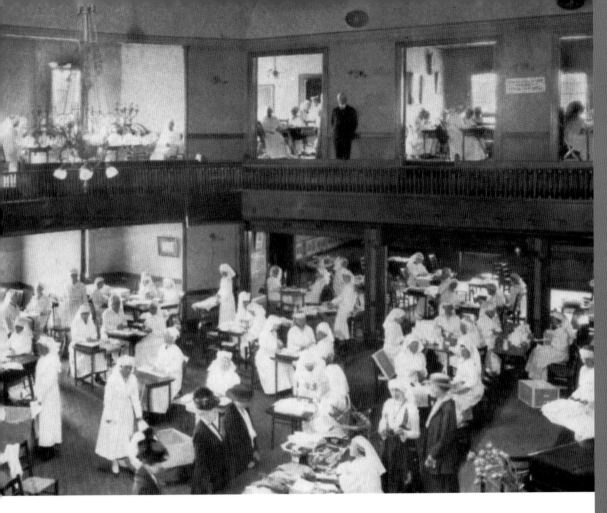

Back home, patriotism took on a theological hue. Dr. Bushnell declared the war a "redemptive cause" for democracy. Even the sanctuary was decked in patriotic garb. Worshipers were constantly reminded of wartime sacrifice by a large banner suspended above the organ, on which a star was placed for every man or woman serving overseas. It was the gift of Mrs. C. J. Winton, whose son David was stationed in France. Two national flags hung on either side, and beside the pulpit stood a cluster of flags from all the Allied nations.

In a public letter dated October 1917 Dr. Bushnell urged servicemen overseas to keep "the fire of the old home religion" burning: "The crowning act of manliness is the calling on the Name of your God, unashamed as one of His sons." He seemed to intuit that this war would change these young people in profound ways: "We want you not only to win your country's fight but your own, and so be able to come back home the same sort of men that you were when you left us, only stronger and better than ever and able to help the rest of us by your witness to the power of God to help men in times of trial and danger." ✛

June 1917	July 1918	November 1918
First U. S. troops arrive in France	Westminster members fight in the Battle of Château-Thierry	War officially ends at 11 a.m. on November 11

MISSIONS TO FOREIGN LANDS

The Woman's Foreign Missionary Society (WFMS) was launched in 1871 when Rev. Robert Sample posed a simple question after one Thursday evening prayer service: "Would you like to help spread the Gospel in foreign lands?" The next day several women appeared at Sample's home to organize a Presbyterian foreign missionary society, the second, after Red Wing, in Minnesota. Foreign mission was women's work in the nineteenth century.

Working through the newly organized Women's Board of the Northwest, the WFMS sent seventy-five dollars the first year toward the support of Miss C. B. Downing in Cheefoo, China. Soon, additional money flowed to missionaries in Africa, Mexico, Siam, Syria, and Persia. By the 1890s membership had grown from the original seven to more than 150, and annual giving climbed to more than three thousand dollars.

By the new century interest in foreign missions was intense. Compelling personal testimonies from missionaries, reinforced by dramatic stories printed in dozens of missionary magazines, fostered a desire in many young people to serve overseas. Young women, both married and single, made up the majority of new missionaries. Their gifts for teaching and nursing were in high demand. A man from the China Inland Mission joked to the WFMS in 1899, "I heard a man from China say that he went . . . talking of missionaries and their wives, but came home talking of missionaries and their husbands. Only women can reach the women of China."

Tales from the mission field brought the world into view. The WFMS joined with other area churches to present lectures, lantern (slide) shows, concerts, and picnics to raise money for special projects, such as the Mateer Hospital in China, made possible by a bequest from Mrs. M. M. Harris in the 1880s. Daughters of the King, a junior mission organization, studied the societies and cultures of different countries in order to understand the missionaries' challenges.

> *In October 1900 Anne Faries recounted stories of the "Chinese Crisis," meaning the Boxer Rebellion. Her brother William Faries and his family escaped unharmed but sent graphic accounts of the destruction wrought by the Boxers, an anti-foreign, anti-Christian secret society nicknamed for their acrobatic moves. Hundreds of missionaries and Chinese Christians were "plundered, beaten, tortured, and killed."*

Giving to foreign missions began to decline nationwide by the 1920s, although not at Westminster. The reasons were varied. While earlier missionary societies were grassroots efforts, run by women at a local level with minimal direction from a central organizing body, a new spirit of efficiency in the 1920s led the General

The Helen Daniels Guild, organized in 1925 in honor of Westminster's missionary to China, helped to support William and Ethel Stoltzfus, who served as Presbyterian missionaries to Syria and Lebanon between 1921 and 1961. The Guild sent boxes of stuffed animals and sewed red play smocks for children at a Presbyterian nursery school in Beirut.

Thousands of Chinese Christians and western missionaries died in the Boxer Rebellion in 1900.

At *left:* The Presbyterian headquarters in Peking fortified with brick, stone, and sandbags.

Above: Ruins of the Presbyterian "Drum Tower" church in Peking.

Assembly to dissolve the regional women's boards and subsume their work under a central, male-run Foreign Missions Board. Individual societies stayed intact, but enthusiasm waned.

Attitudes had changed. The young women of the 1920s were "a generation looking with unafraid eyes at all institutions, even ecclesiastical—and asking 'why?' of many accepted customs," noted Katherine Jones Bennett, an early Presbyterian executive. This new generation was reluctant to join their mothers' organizations. "Missionary societies had become so tightly organized that unless you knew the exact language and followed the rules, it wasn't very interesting," one young woman commented.

Westminster bucked this trend, at least for a while, with new organizations that generated camaraderie and fired up young women's imaginations. A chapter of Westminster Guild, organized in 1918 for "young ladies over 18," focused on "study, service, worship, and recreation." When the young ladies aged out, they changed their name to Westminster Service Guild and kept their group going. Membership peaked in 1949 at 203. The Junior Missionary Society, begun in 1925, gave more direct attention to

missions and changed its name to the Helen Daniels Missionary Society in 1926 to honor a missionary they supported. Dr. Bushnell called it "a power house in the church" in the late 1930s.

Mission giving at Westminster also flourished in the 1920s and early 1930s. The high water mark relative to other churches in the denomination was set in 1922 when Rev. John Bushnell accepted an award at the General Assembly in Philadelphia that recognized Westminster and its women for raising $17,986.84, more than any other Presbyterian church in the United States.

In her 1968 mimeographed history of the Westminster Service Guild, Francys E. Shull recalls the enthusiasm of the 1920s: "The years 1920 to 1925 were wonderful ones in which to be a young missionary society in Westminster Church. The war was a thing of the past. Prohibition and woman's suffrage (both causes for which Westminster women had worked long and hard) had become the law of the land. At last it seemed church women had time and energy to spare, and they turned joyously to renewed and expanded missionary activity." ✦

"To leave one's own four walls and surrounding garden these days is to go from peace into war and with the terrible control which is exercised by those in authority over all products and the prices of necessities up so high that the usual wage does not even cover the price of rice.... We all have to give and give of our own salaries in order to help our workers." (September 26, 1940)

Missionary hardships HELEN DANIELS

The hardships of missionary life are well illustrated in Helen Daniels's experience. Described as "charming, vivacious, happy and alert," she arrived in Nanking with her husband, Dr. John Horton Daniels, in September 1919. Except for occasional furloughs, she remained in China through the late 1940s. Her medical files, diligently kept by the Foreign Mission Board, reveal the physical challenges she and her family faced. Daniels safely delivered her first child in China, but after an appendectomy she had to abort the next. She returned to the United States to bear her next two while John remained behind. Her children were frequently sick. Her daughter Harriet, for example, survived tonsillitis, mumps, measles, whooping cough, scarlet fever, and bronchial pneumonia before returning to Minnesota to attend Carleton College in 1938. Daniels herself was never in vigorous health. Medical reports testify to her constant struggles with fatigue. By November 1941 she was suffering mentally, fearing constantly for her husband, who remained in China while she spent the war years in Minneapolis. Under care for anxiety, she recovered and left for China in 1946.

Daniels's letters provide a fascinating glimpse into China's changing political landscape:

"I wish to convey . . . some of the thrill which has been ours during these last exciting weeks here in China when history was in the making. You have read the facts in your papers, how Chiang Kai-shek was captured, held and finally released on Christmas Day, but even the most versatile reporter could not convey the atmosphere . . . vibrating with excitement, loyalty and spontaneous patriotism . . . . The story which you may have heard, that General Chiang . . . asked for only one thing, his Bible, is a substantiated fact." (February 14, 1937) ✛

A desire to serve EDNA BISSELL

WOMAN'S FOREIGN MISSIONARY SOCIETY
OF THE
PRESBYTERY OF MINNEAPOLIS.

Minneapolis, Minn., Oct 3rd 1896.

A Family Commitment:
The Faries Family

For the family of Isaiah C. Faries, mission work was a family affair. The commitment began with Mrs. Faries, who became Westminster's first WFMS president while her husband served as the pastor of Franklin Avenue Presbyterian Church. Their eldest son, Dr. William Faries, described as "a cripple" and "somewhat dwarfed in nature," graduated from New York Medical College, married, and in 1889 went to Wei Hein, China, as a medical missionary. His accounts of the Boxer Rebellion enthralled Westminster's members. The younger son, John, became a minister at Hope Chapel before moving to other pastorates around the United States. Daughter Anne was the first treasurer of the Minneapolis branch of the Waldensian Aid Society, which partnered with Westminster in the 1920s-30s to send aid to political and religious refugees in Europe. Other families at Westminster showed similar patterns, with several generations devoting themselves to church work.

Above: A letter of recommendation for Edna Bissell written by Mrs. Helen Williams, president of the Presbytery-wide Woman's Foreign Missionary Society, in October 1896.

At right: A typical foreign mission pledge card, ca. 1898.

Edna Iola Bissell's mother died young, her brothers moved west, and her obligations to her father ended with his death in 1896. Without family ties or marriage prospects, this thirty-year-old Westminster member with "a winning smile" was open to adventure. Inspired by the tales she heard as a child from her uncle, Dr. Lemuel Bissell, a Presbyterian missionary to India, she applied for support to the Woman's Foreign Missionary Society. "My whole heart turns longing to be used in His service where He may lead," she wrote in her application essay. Her high school diploma, excellent recommendations, musical talent, and several years' teaching experience at Riverside Chapel were enough to secure her a position as a missionary teacher at the Harriet House School in Bangkok. She departed for Siam on September 11, 1899.

Mrs. Frank Daniels of the WFMS reported on Edna Bissell's situation: "The Harriet House School . . . is one of the most comfortable and best schools on the field, but one of the hardest. There are eighty girls and two teachers. It is a city school and the girls are never allowed to go off their rather limited play-grounds even for a walk. The river runs in front and on that they are sometimes permitted to ride. All other times they see nothing beyond the high stone walls. These girls are from the higher classes . . . . The Siamese nobility and European residents form a little social life about our missionary, where her power to attract, and her musical ability greatly extends her influence." Sadly, Edna Bissell fell ill and returned to the United States in 1906 and died the following year. ✠

The Offerings and Subscriptions To-day

WILL BE OUR ANNUAL OFFERING FOR

The Board of Foreign Missions.

Please designate your subscription (payable before next April) as indicated below.

I hereby pledge $_____ Will Pay_____

Do you wish envelopes for periodical payments?_____

Name_____

Address_____

Subscriptions are payable to Chas. H. Curtis, Treas. of Benevolences.

The coming new religion

FUNDAMENTALISM VS. MODERNISM

Top: Westminster youth form their own "militant suffragist" parade in Glenwood Park, 1913.

Above: Miss Maude Royden, the famous assistant pastor of London's City Temple, preached at Westminster in 1923 on "The World at the Crossroads."

The 1920s-30s were not happy times for the Presbyterian Church in the U.S.A. With World War I barely over, the denomination lurched into a new conflict between fundamentalism and modernism, with opposing camps battling over issues of theology, polity, and the role of Christianity in public life. These issues found their way to Westminster's door, as Rev. John Bushnell preached sermons with such titles as "The Coming New Religion," "Things Above Debate," and "Don't Burn Your Bible."

Dr. Bushnell's congregation lived in a world very different from that of Westminster's founders. Urban growth and commercial development brought new secularizing trends. Sunday ball games, newspapers, theater productions, rail travel, and country club gatherings all threatened the sacred status of Sunday church services and signaled a move away from traditional Protestant values. Some comfort came from the tremendous growth of the major Protestant denominations, which tripled in membership from five to sixteen million between 1860 and 1900. But Bushnell knew that religion was exerting a smaller and smaller influence on large arenas of American life. >>>

1859	1892	1920
Darwin publishes *The Origin of Species*	General Assembly (GA) endorses doctrine of biblical inerrancy	The term "fundamentalism" coined

"Move out into its tall timber. View its majesties. Be still among its sublime graces. Breathe its balsam. Hark to the music of its orchestral boughs. . . . Walk out in the great forest of God and you will find Him there . . . . What perplexities remain for you in the Book are but in the shrubbery."

Rev. John Edward Bushnell, "But Don't Burn Your Bible," sermon preached September 18, 1927

>>>

New ideas also threatened Christian orthodoxy. Darwin's evolutionary hypothesis challenged biblical accounts of creation; higher criticism of the Bible undermined Mosaic authorship of the Pentateuch; the rise of social sciences, such as anthropology, sociology, and comparative religions raised questions about absolute truth. Karl Marx's famous observation "All that is solid melts into air" might well have applied to Christian belief. Could Westminster's members still believe in the inerrancy of Scripture?

Vigorous debates arose among Presbyterians over how to respond to these challenges. New Theology, also known as modernism or liberalism, sought to reconcile the old faith with new realities. Inspired by the Social Gospel movements of the late nineteenth century, New Theology emphasized the immanence of God, the goodness of humanity, and the importance of personal experience and ethics in religion. Harry Emerson Fosdick, who preached at Westminster in January 1919, became one of modernism's most famous proponents. His 1922 sermon "Shall the Fundamentalists Win?" provoked conservatives to orchestrate his resignation from the Presbyterian Church, after which he continued preaching his "intelligent understanding of Biblical materials" at New York's Riverside Church and Union Theological Seminary.

On the opposing side were "fundamentalists," led by such figures as William Jennings Bryan, Presbyterian elder and three-time candidate for President of the United States. They espoused the "fundamentals of faith": the literal interpretation of the Bible, a rigid

approach to salvation, and staunch opposition to historical analysis in biblical exegesis. For several years in the early 1920s fundamentalists maintained the upper hand in the denomination, and Bryan was nearly elected Moderator of the General Assembly in 1923. But his poor performance at the Scopes trial in Dayton, Tennessee, confirmed stereotypes of fundamentalists as ignorant, narrow-minded, and reactionary, and by the late 1920s the liberals had assumed leadership, if not intellectual victory.

Dr. Bushnell steered Westminster on a moderate course. He preferred to watch the theological battles from the sidelines and encouraged his congregation to explore the issues for themselves. As other Minneapolis churches took positions on the debates, he quietly held steady. Bushnell continued to nurture Westminster's close relationship with Plymouth Congregational Church, which became a center of theological liberalism under the leadership of the Reverend Harry Dewey. Yet Dr. Bushnell also continued to support gospel revivals in collaboration with some of the city's more conservative congregations, such as First Baptist Church where the fiery Reverend William Bell Riley emerged as one of the nation's most forceful advocates of fundamentalism. "Read if you will your newest books and authors," Bushnell advised his congregation, "but don't burn your Bibles." In that stance, he anticipated the more conciliatory neo-orthodox theology that was to guide Presbyterians through the mid-twentieth century. ✛

From William Jennings Bryan, *Seven Questions in Dispute*, 1924.

1922
Rev. Harry Emerson Fosdick ignites debates with sermon "Shall the Fundamentalists Win?"

1925
Trial of John Scopes for teaching of evolution ends in symbolic defeat for fundamentalists

1926
Special GA Commission declares "fundamentals" non-binding and guarantees tolerance for liberal evangelicals

71

A SKELETON IN THE CLOSET

To the Session and congregation of Westminster Presbyterian Church of Minneapolis Minn. Feby 15th 1932

I hereby tender my resignation as minister of Westminster church to take effect immediately —

Edwin F. Rippey.

When the committee that wrote *A Telling Presence* in 1982 heard the rattling of bones in a church closet, they cracked the door enough to let a hint slip out. Intervening events make airing skeletons a wiser choice. How Westminster has dealt with scandal is a legitimate subject for historical inquiry.

The first fifteen months of the Reverend Edwin F. Rippey's tenure, from Oct. 2, 1930, looked promising. The Deacons' mission of hospitality had been rejuvenated; young people's programs flourished, and Dr. Rippey's energy for pastoral care "much impressed" the Session.

> *Then, in February 1932, Dr. Rippey was caught in an extramarital affair. The few church officers informed spun into action to dismiss him and keep the offense secret. A handscrawled letter of resignation dated February 15 now lies in a box of random documents in the church attic.*

The next evening the elders were called into Session in the pastor's study. Dr. Rippey opened with prayer, then "spoke about the difficulties of his office and of his increasing sense of unfitness for the Pastorate of Westminster and his final conviction that the best interests of the Church would be served better by someone other than himself. He stated that the matter was not open to discussion and that his decision was irrevocable." Session granted him an immediate leave of absence.

After the scheduled election of officers at the February 25 congregational meeting, a different letter of resignation, dated February 22, was tendered: "After an exhaustive examination by the most competent diagnosticians, I have been advised to leave immediately for a much milder and equable climate."

With spring just a month away, Minnesota's winter took the rap. Pastor Emeritus John Bushnell, called back to work, "made an earnest plea for the wholehearted efforts and unified action of the Congregation."

Presbytery received the request to suspend the pastoral relationship on March 7 and asked that all papers related to the matter be sealed and filed. The February 15 letter was obviously omitted.

Secrecy did not make the pesky matter go away. On May 5 an officer from First Presbyterian Church of Phoenix wrote that they were considering a call to Dr. Rippey. "Of course, a large church like ours, with its many problems, would not consider engaging as our regular pastor a man that was not in the best of health," he hinted. Clerk of Session Edward S. Smith responded, "His resignation was requested for causes the nature of which could best be ascertained by you through a personal visit to our City." If his ministry depended on a reference from Westminster, Rippey was effectively put to pasture at forty-seven.

When the Reverend William H. Boddy was presented to the congregation in August, five members of the nominating committee testified to his virtues. The committee's investigations had been "exhaustive and many-sided" and had found Dr. Boddy to have "a personal character that is above reproach."

Dr. Boddy understood the need for caution. He asked Session to name two members to investigate his personal appointments. Session asked him "to restrict his activities to Westminster Church exclusively for at least the first part of his ministry, in order that his strength and energy might be conserved for the work of the parish." A parish left in the whisper-filled dark no doubt needed careful tending. ✝

Men wait for a meal at the Union City Mission, 1924. The Mission's farm on Medicine Lake was used as a sort of safety valve during the bread riots in 1931. Hundreds of hungry men were bussed there to keep them off the city streets, where they might join in the protests.

SPENT, BEWILDERED, AND HOPELESS

Because Westminster built a chapel and a parish house in 1937, we might assume that the church was spared the hardship of the Great Depression. It fared remarkably well, but only with careful stewardship of the budget. Staff salaries and annual budgets were trimmed back on occasion, mainly because pew rentals and offerings fell short. Rupert Sircom, organist and choirmaster, was asked more than once to practice restraint in spending for the music program.

The decline in income suggests that members of the congregation had their own struggles. A clearinghouse to match out-of-work members with potential employers was proposed in 1931, but no evidence has turned up to show whether and how it worked. Westminster kept tabs on Riverside Chapel's congregation. Of its 501 members, 72 identified themselves as on relief in 1938, and others might not have come forward.

Hard times show up in language as well as numbers. Herman Sweet's exemplary youth programs didn't shy away from tough topics. A 1936 invitation to the Fireside Society, the post-high school group, begins, "In this period of confused living and chaotic thinking." A 1935 appeal to the congregation from the Board of Trustees calls the church "a real bulwark in these difficult times against the forces of anarchy, evil and pessimism which are doing their best to destroy society and religion."

The "forces" referred to included Communism in Russia and Nazism in Germany but also local events that stirred red scares. The passage of the National Industrial Recovery Act of 1933, which secured workers' right to collective bargaining, set off a flurry of union organizing vigorously opposed by business groups represented in Westminster's congregation. A series of strikes by the Teamsters Union kept downtown embattled through >>>

Rev. William H. Boddy, Westminster's Pastor, 1932-40.

the spring and summer of 1934. On July 20 police fired on a demonstration turned riotous at Third Street and Sixth Avenue North, killing two pickets and wounding sixty-seven other people. Rev. William H. Boddy, characterized as an advocate for social justice, supported collective bargaining and the right to picket. He served on the Commission of Public Affairs of the Minneapolis Ministers' Federation, which tried in vain to reconcile the opposing sides and to get them to agree to arbitration.

Dr. Boddy's sermons, letters, and prayers set a tone of somber yearning, as illustrated in this undated Advent prayer: "Come, thou Christ of Bethlehem, to our world spent, bewildered, and hopeless. Come, deliver us from the tomb of deadening despairs. Help us to believe again in Love and all its healing power. Let the angels' song of peace and good will become the haunting hope and authentic ambition of every ruler and legislator and citizen. Come to our darkening world. No light but Thine can pierce this gloom. Even now let Thy star appear, Thy heavens open; Thine angels sing."

Ill health shadowed Dr. Boddy through much of his tenure. In September 1939 he obtained a six-month leave to be treated for leukemia at Abbott Hospital. A brand new assistant pastor, James E. Waery, was "placed in full authority over the affairs of the Church." Members not only donated money to pay for their "Beloved

Minister's" care but gave blood to support his many transfusions. Questions about his prognosis must have been sensitive: The February 1940 Session meeting delegated two elders who were absent to consult with him

about his plans. The leave was extended, and on April 4, 1940, Dr. Boddy resigned in an eloquent letter to the congregation in which he offered this "gratuitous advice":

> "There is for Westminster Church just one place of leadership. She must give to the city a ministry that is warmly evangelical but which is also scholarly and modern-minded. She must find a minister who ever calls people to new adventures with Christ in personal living and to the daring application of the timeless insights of Jesus to the problems of collective living. For Westminster to fail to furnish such leadership means she merely duplicates what other churches are doing adequately and fails in her own great opportunity."

He died sixteen days later at fifty-four. Dr. William Chalmers Covert, a retired church executive who had been ordained at Westminster, filled the pulpit until Dr. Arnold Lowe arrived. Mr. Waery went his own way in June 1941 after as rigorous training in tall-steeple parish ministry as any assistant has likely received. ✢

1929
New York stock market crashes in October

1931
Food riots in Minneapolis: crowds smashing grocery store windows are brought under control by more than 100 policemen

1932
Revenue Act of 1932 raises top tax rates from 25 to 63 percent

Far left: The Union City Mission at Hennepin Avenue and Second Street, 1936.

Near left: The Memorial Day parade passes Westminster in 1937.

Above: Police use teargas to disperse a crowd downtown during the Teamsters strike of 1934, which involved drivers of delivery trucks and elicited sympathy strikes in the building trades. This event was a turning point for Minneapolis, where business had been especially resistant to labor unions. Aided by new legislation, as well, truckers won the right to organize, and workers in other industries soon followed suit. Dr. Boddy, who supported collective bargaining, faced a congregation no doubt divided on how to apply Christian faith to volatile issues of social class.

1933	**1934**	**1935**	**1936**	**1938**	**1939**
President Roosevelt begins to implement "The New Deal"	Minneapolis Teamsters strike leads to fierce fighting between strikers and police	Social Security Act passed	Temperatures in Minnesota remain below zero for a record thirty-six days	Fair Labor Standards Act passed, enacting first national minimum wage	Westminster suspends its Sunday evening service

GEORGE DRAPER DAYTON'S CHALLENGE

Even as the Depression eroded Westminster's operating budget, the church's programs flourished. Youth activities, drama productions, women's organizations, scouts, and timely adult education classes provided wholesome opportunities for budget-conscious families. The problem was finding space for everything.

In February 1934 Dr. Boddy asked the Trustees to consider financing an addition to the church. Too many groups met in private homes, he said, which was "not ideal from the viewpoint of making the Church the center of all activities." Perhaps a modest addition could meet the church's needs for the next decade. The tract of land behind the church on Marquette Avenue had been purchased in 1923 for just this purpose, but building had been postponed.

The Trustees were understandably cautious. Income from pew rentals had dropped from a high of $16,500 to $12,500 in 1933, the overall budget had shrunk about 20 percent, and investment income was unpredictable. But a series of bequests to Westminster had enlarged the endowment and could provide several thousand dollars in ready cash. Eager to move forward, Dr. Boddy brought architect Thomas Tallmadge to the Trustees' April 1934 meeting. They liked his plans and approved a small addition to the Sunday school rooms. Curiosity led the Trustees to request additional sketches for a full parish house so they could imagine what might come in the future. Once viewed, these plans were hard to resist. But what about the money?

George Draper Dayton stepped in with a challenge: If the congregation could raise $225,000, the Dayton Foundation would contribute $100,000 toward the building of a parish house and an endowment for its maintenance. "Angels do not come visibly to earth to lead us out; God chooses men," Pastor Emeritus John Bushnell wrote of Dayton's proposition. Dayton had only >>>

Groups at Westminster in 1935

prior to the construction of the Parish House:

Church Boards
Boy Scouts
Girl Scouts
Church School
Choirs
Fireside Groups
Fellowship Club

Men's Groups
Men's Fellowship
Men's Chorus

Women's Association
Helen Daniels Guild
Westminster Service Guild
Mother's Club
Women's Missionary Department
Social Service Department
Abbott Hospital Auxiliary
Amico Club

George Draper Dayton's challenge to the congregation in 1934 resulted in Westminster's chapel, dedicated in 1937, featuring a striking Gothic design reputed to be the preference of his daughter-in-law Grace Bliss Dayton.

recently joined the church. His sons' families had played larger roles at Westminster than he and his wife, Emma, had. Nearing his eightieth year, he knew this might be his final act in a long life of benevolence. His father's service as a Presbyterian elder had inspired a lifelong love for the church. As a boy Dayton had hoped to become a minister, but God called him into business, he claimed. His vocation was to tithe regularly and generously.

Dayton first came to Minnesota from upstate New York in 1883 to assume the leadership of a failing Worthington bank. He and Emma raised their family in Worthington's Westminster Presbyterian Church, where George served as an elder and led services on occasion when no minister was available. Careful stewardship and wise business practices enhanced his reputation. As his businesses prospered, he invested in Minneapolis real estate, buying Westminster's Seventh Street property after the fire in 1895 and opening a dry goods store on the spot in 1902. When the family moved to Minneapolis, George and Emma joined First

Presbyterian Church, while their sons, David and George Nelson Dayton, came to Westminster. David served as the church's auditor and an elder until his early death in 1923; David's wife led Daughters of the King and the Woman's Foreign Missionary Society. George Nelson also served as an elder before moving to the Board of Trustees. George Draper and Emma followed their sons to Westminster in 1925. The entire family drew admiration and respect for their devotion to the church.

The congregation responded swiftly to Dayton's challenge, raising $237,673 within two weeks. With Dayton's gift and additional pledges, a total of $404,000 was available for new Sunday school rooms and meeting spaces, as well as a beautiful chapel. The chapel's expensive Gothic design was heavily influenced by his daughter-in-law Grace Bliss Dayton, her sons maintained. The architectural firm of Magney and Tusler drew up final plans, and dirt began to fly in September 1936. The new chapel was dedicated in October 1937, barely two months after Westminster's eightieth anniversary. "Altars are made out of anointed stones, but the most sacred shrines are created out of the rough stuff of human experiences lifted to God and blessed by him," Dr. Boddy declared at the service.

George Draper Dayton lived just a few months more, long enough to donate additional money toward the purchase of 1,500 new hymnals for the sanctuary and chapel. Current Westminster member Bruce Dayton wrote a dedication in his grandfather's biography, *A Man of Parts,* that might well serve as a memorial for the chapel: "To the fulfillment of George Draper Dayton's oft-repeated petition that 'my descendants to the latest generation may know and love God.'" ✛

The Dayton family gathered at the Minneapolis home of George Draper and Emma Willard Chadwick Dayton *(back row, right)* about 1925.

SCOUTING

Troop 33, the oldest continuous Boy Scout troop in the Twin Cities metropolitan area, formed in 1918 while war was raging in Europe. The impetus came from Earl Haverstock, an attorney for The Minnesota Loan and Trust Company, who believed scouting would be "a good thing for the boy, the scoutmaster, the community, and the country." The initial group of twenty-seven maintained a junior service flag modeled after the World War I service flag at the front of Westminster's sanctuary.

Offering a wider variety of activities than the popular YMCA, Scouts aimed to develop character and foster a desire for national and community service. Athletics, games, and camping honed their physical beings. "Our troop's marching and drill activities became famous," Milton Thompson remembered. Along with scouts from Hennepin Avenue Methodist Church, Troop 33 dominated the annual citywide scout competition known as Wali-ga-zhu. First aid, knot tying, Morse code, and signaling were their specialties.

The Depression fed the Boy Scouts' popularity. A waiting list developed for the troop's sixty-four spots, and Cub Pack 3 was added in 1932. The large numbers created certain challenges. Scoutmaster Kyle Cudworth often shared the story of when, in the midst of the era's privations, George Dayton offered to help the troop with transportation to Wali-ga-zhu. A procession of chauffered limousines and Cadillacs arrived at the church on loan from Dayton's Wayzata friends. With no other option, the scouts reluctantly climbed in and took a razzing from the other troops for their extravagance.

The Girl Scouts, Troop 3 and later Troop 153, reached Westminster in the mid-1920s and thrived in the 1930s under the >>>

Scouting aims to develop a range of skills in young people.
Above: Westminster Girl Scouts run races outside the church.
At left: Members of Troop 33 join together in song.

leadership of Mrs. Herman (Alfra) Sweet and Rewey Belle Inglis. Their activities included sewing and knitting for missions, as well as study of astronomy, dance, mapping, hiking, and first aid. The Girl Scouts' annual citywide competition, Gymkhana, featured a costume parade: "My troop went as a sewing basket, and I was a needle. Other people were pincushions and things like that. It was exciting," Barbara Knight Coffin remembers.

Both troops floundered during World War II when their leaders went overseas for service in the military or Red Cross. Wartime shortages compounded the problem. "Families weren't willing to spend the gasoline. Everyone was conserving and of course they came from all over, the same as they do now," Betty Bryan explains. The Girl Scouts regrouped for a short time after the war and began serving at the Thursday night suppers. "With great pride we wore our baggy green uniforms, all of our badges, frequently with a knife and a compass dangling from belt hooks. Often have I wondered what the diners thought of their overdressed waitresses!" Bryan exclaims. While they delivered hot meals to tables of hungry congregants, Dr. Lowe gave his weekly book reviews.

Sadly, the Girl Scouts folded sometime in the 1950s but returned for a brief stint in the 1990s. Troop 33 continues today and has been joined by Troop 100, the world's first Hmong Boy Scout troop. ✣

Above: Scouts in the dining hall at Camp Ajawah.

At right: Scoutmaster Dave Moore with Va Vang, Doua Xiong, Koua Her, and Kao Vang.

HOPE IN HARD TIMES

CAMP AJAWAH

Our whole family grew up at Ajawah," Gina Gustavson says of her childhood in the 1950s. "There's something about Ajawah that gets in your blood. You can be there with people all around and find a quiet place to withdraw and meditate and just enjoy being in nature." Generations of children have shared similar memories and will continue to do so.

Camp Ajawah dates back to 1918 when Troop 33 started camping in dormitory-style buildings on Phelps Island in Lake Minnetonka. The camp moved in the early 1920s to facilities on nearby Lake Sarah. As the area developed, the camp routine included assigning the regular nighttime guard to walk the perimeter of the grounds to keep out people who had been drinking. Eager for a more peaceful and remote site, Westminster's Trustees signed a lease in May 1929 for a twenty-eight-acre camp with fifteen hundred feet of shoreline on Linwood Lake, six miles west of Wyoming, a small town just north of the Twin Cities. Westminster purchased the land in 1958 and nearly doubled its size in 1978 with a twenty-two-acre memorial to Kyle Cudworth, Ajawah's long-time camp director. Programs catered to boys and girls, scouts and non-scouts.

The name "Camp Ajawah" reflects the scouts' interest in newfangled technology. In the early 1920s the Boy Scouts operated an amateur (ham) radio station in the basement of the church with a call sign of W9AJA. Taking the AJA of their station and joining it with the AWA of Camp Tonkawa, the Minneapolis Scout Council's camp on Lake Minnetonka, they created Ajawah. The name traveled with them from one campsite to the next.

Today Ajawah is run by a camping board with members drawn from Westminster's congregation and beyond. As the camp moves into the future, there are ongoing issues to resolve, such as how to nurture Westminster children's faith development while also welcoming a broader community of campers, and how to meet current standards of safety and accessibility without diminishing the camp's rustic appeal. >>>

At left and above: Swimmers at Camp Ajawah, carefully protected by life jackets, test the waters of Linwood Lake.

At left: Picture-taking time. Campers sleep in heavy, rustic tents on platforms.

Below, from top:
Clowning around in the girl's camp, June 2006.

Back to the tent after beaching the canoe.

Flag ceremonies are an important part of the day at Ajawah.

"One year there was a tame deer living just behind the Scout Line. Some people called him Fred and other people, Clyde. Still others called him Fred-or-Clyde. He thought he was one of the kids, and when Assembly blew for Retreat, he would go running down to the Flats to line up with everyone else. He could never figure out why we wouldn't let him into the Mess Hall to eat with us. And he wasn't very patriotic. While the guys were trying to salute the flag, he would be prancing around and bumping up against them, asking for attention. We never saw him after that one summer. I suppose in the fall he walked up to a hunter to say hello."
Dave Moore, current camp director, recalling the 1940s.

"The dancing flames of the camp fire lighted the intent faces of some forty campers as they listened to Chief Esmond Avery recount the 'Legend of the Mysterious Grave.' Waves lapped gently on the beach of Lake Sarah, and the leaves of the sugar maple trees whispered overhead. Chief Esmond told how two surveyors planning the route of the first railroad in that area had been murdered and their bodies buried somewhere near Camp Ajawah. An award awaited the camper who first found 'The Mysterious Grave.' The first moment I heard the story, 'The Mysterious Grave' became my quest for the Holy Grail, and during the summers of 1924 through 1928 I spent every minute of free time searching through the woods of Camp Ajawah for it. In the process, I became a life long naturalist."
Charles B. Reif, one of Ajawah's first campers and camp director, 1955-56.

"People can live side by side and work side by side regardless of who they are or what they are in the rest of the world. You could have a person coming from a family who lives in a fancy house on Lake Harriet or Lake of the Isles and someone coming from the inner city who is there on a scholarship. And they could be campers together and be friends, and the differences that might exist in the other world don't exist at Ajawah."
Gina McCabe Gustavson, who attended Camp Ajawah in the 1950s-60s and returned as a counselor in her teen years and as camp nurse in her adulthood.

SAFE HAVEN

"When men, therefore, say that these are the worst times, we must counter with the insistence that in the worst times we must stand for the best things . . . . Let us stand for the moral principles of Jesus."

Dr. Arnold H. Lowe, "Standing for the Best Things in the Worst Times," sermon preached on October 11, 1942

Bill and Ellen McCabe head to a worship service with their four children, Steve, Rick, Gina, and Gil, 1955. The angle of the photo doesn't reveal that baby Becky is on the way.

A preacher for the times
THE REVEREND ARNOLD LOWE

In any institution's history, certain figures tower above the rest. For Westminster, that person is the Reverend Doctor Arnold Hilmar Lowe, pastor from 1941 to 1965. A powerful preacher with national stature, he presided over the church during World War II and its conservative aftermath, retiring just as President Lyndon Johnson's Great Society was taking hold.

When he arrived in the United States from Switzerland at seventeen in 1905, he viewed America as "the promised land," a place of hope and opportunity where people could remake themselves. After attending Bloomfield College in New Jersey, he graduated from the College of Wooster and earned a Master of Arts from Western Theological Seminary in Pittsburgh. In characteristically vigorous fashion, he pursued a mission post in Cameroon after his ordination in 1912. Military service in Europe followed, and then a teaching post at Missouri Valley College, where he met his wife, Braddie. He served nearly fourteen years as pastor of the Kingshighway Presbyterian Church in St. Louis before coming to Westminster in April 1941.

"A pastor, theologian, ecclesiastical statesman and creative writer, he was also a business executive, custodian of vast funds, and psychiatrist," Mary Mitchell wrote in a profile for the *Minneapolis Sunday Tribune.* Without question, though, Lowe's forte was preaching. "It was—well, I'm running out of adjectives on the plus side—it was brilliant," Herb Bissell remembers. "He held people's attention with a striking, forceful voice and manner. . . . I found him very, very stimulating." Lorraine Purdy agrees, "You always went home with something to think about." >>>

When Arnold Lowe spoke at McCormick Seminary in the late 1960s shortly after his retirement from Westminster, his reputation was announced in whispers across campus: "Pope Lowe is coming to town!"

Hymn-singing in the 1960s.

Westminster membership over the years

Year	Membership
1947	3,183
1957	3,980
1967	3,751
1977	2,832
1987	3,191
1997	2,816
2007	2,929

A sampling of Arnold Lowe's books

The Glow and the Glory

Guidelines to Courageous Living

Beliefs Have Consequences

The Importance of Being Ourselves

Start Where You Are

The Worth of a Man

When God Moves In

Power for Life's Living

>>>

His sermons, simple when read, rang with gravity and prophetic vision when delivered. Using declarative sentences, few adjectives, and sparse metaphors, he exhorted worshipers to pursue lives of purpose and reflection. "In contrast to the life-is-wonderful advocates, he has the courage to say that life is difficult," one contemporary observed. Over and again he called for "responsibility in an irresponsible age" and a "reawakening of moral conscience." He targeted tough topics like bigotry, militarism, and capitalist greed in precisely chosen words. "Some burned, some stung, some encouraged."

Named "preacher of the year" in 1956 by the Presbyterian General Assembly, Dr. Lowe was invited to address the National Presbyterian Church in Washington, D.C., where President Dwight Eisenhower and Secretary of State John Foster Dulles worshiped. He directed his remarks to government officials: "A man's public service is an act of consecration, as it was when Isaiah said, 'Here am I; send me.' You who stand in the arena of public service must feel yourselves compelled by God, no less than those who stand in the pulpits of their churches."

Described as "an intellectual point man for the community," he added countless civic duties to his demanding schedule. In addition to serving on the boards of Macalester College, the Community Chest, and the Red Cross, he drew hundreds to his annual book nights at the Minneapolis Club, where he would dispense pithy remarks on a long list of his favorite titles. His appetite for books was widely known. Reading 1,500 words a minute (the average is 300), he consumed 150 to 175 titles a year that ranged from history and biography to mystery and fiction. Not content to be a mere reader, he also authored twenty books. His collection of sermons, *Start Where You Are,* sold 14,300 copies in the first year—a record, according to his publishers—and contributed to the growing popularity of inspirational literature. Somehow he also found time for golf.

SAFE HAVEN

" 'Tell me this, Mrs. Nelson, do you believe that Jesus was the Son of God?' She looked at him and said, 'Dr. Lowe, I believe that Jesus was a son of God.' He kind of leaned back, thought for a minute and said, 'Well, I guess that is okay.'"

Under his leadership Westminster grew more formal. He supervised the remodeling of the chancel in 1943 to include a fixed pulpit, smaller platform, and massive chairs for the ministers, all skirted by a low railing. Decorum was the goal. "From now on, the ministers need no longer be embarrassed, wondering what to do with their feet," he wrote in a letter. A new grille covered the organ pipes so "those who come to church from now on can spend much less time counting." The architectural changes centered attention on the preacher and lent an air of dignity. It was quite a change from the days of Rev. David James Burrell.

The new conservatism suited the times. Lowe's own politics emphasized individual responsibility and personal morality. Communism was evil, and community building, with its overtones of collectivism, was not yet the popular topic it is today. God, country, and family were his grand themes. "Arnold did not resist change casually," Bissell muses. His leadership style tended toward the autocratic and perfectionist. He dominated all that went on at Westminster and had little use for wider governing bodies like the presbytery. While some may have chafed, others held him in awe.

Reflecting nationwide trends in churchgoing, Westminster prospered in the 1950s, providing a haven in an uncertain post-war world. Lowe devoted many hours to personal counseling, a new trend in the inward-turning, therapeutically-minded 1950s, and drew in hundreds of new members in the process. Never has the church been so consistently packed on Sunday mornings. Membership soared from 2,359 to 3,700 between 1941 and 1951 and topped out at 3,980 in 1957. Pledges followed suit. >>>

Conversations with Dr. Lowe could be intense, and he insisted on meeting with every prospective member. Lorraine Purdy quaked at the thought of speaking with him during her new member interview in 1948: "I knew how kind he was, but he scared me." For all his strong convictions Lowe was not dogmatic and could surprise people with his openness. Former Clerk of Session Art Nelson recounts the story of his mother's interview in the 1940s. During their conservation Lowe discovered that she held some rather unorthodox ideas, including some of her Swedish father's Theosophical beliefs: "He finally got down to saying, 'Tell me this, Mrs. Nelson, do you believe that Jesus was the Son of God?' She looked at him and said, 'Dr. Lowe, I believe that Jesus was *a* son of God.' He kind of leaned back, thought for a minute and said, 'Well, I guess that is okay.'"

>>>

By the 1960s urban flight and suburban sprawl posed new problems, but these would be for Lowe's successors to face. "The pastor of a great downtown church in any large American city faces a challenge," the *Tribune* columnist George Grim, a Westminster elder, wrote in October 1964. "Often, the edifice is surrounded by office buildings, hotels, motels, parking lots, convention facilities. The families and their children have moved to farther reaches of the city, out to the suburbs. How to keep such a church meaningful, needed, is an insistent problem." Westminster was well poised to meet these challenges.

Above: Sunday attendance hit an all-time high in the mid-1950s. Here, the congregation departs after worship, 1956. Note the Lyceum Theater where Orchestra Hall now stands.

Dr. Lowe reluctantly retired in April 1965 at the age of seventy-six. His valedictory sermon, "The Sum and Substance of It All," was heard by a standing-room-only crowd and broadcast on KRSI radio. Loudspeakers carried his voice from the sanctuary to the chapel, Great Hall, and all parts of the building, where 2,500 people filled even the staircases. It happened to be the first Sunday Jim and Carmen Campbell attended Westminster:

"We got there a little late, and no seats were available except in the aisles of the balcony. It's a good thing the fire department didn't know the church was that packed. There wasn't a dry eye in the house that day. It was an incredibly emotional experience, and we've been sitting in the balcony ever since." ✛

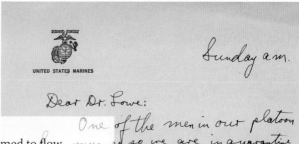

Arnold Lowe was a prodigious writer. His words seemed to flow effortlessly, whether in sermons, books, or letters. Several times a year, aided by a mimeograph machine, he sent greetings to individual members, often with personal notations. During World War II his letters traveled the globe, ministering to servicemen and women stationed everywhere from Italy to India, North Africa to the Pacific.

The United States entered the war just months after Dr. Lowe arrived at Westminster. Any doubts about the loyalty of this German-accented immigrant were quickly dispelled by his vehement rhetoric. "Pearl Harbor does not belong to any political party. It belongs to you and to me," he declared at a war rally. "You and I cannot stand by idly. We cannot simply fold our hands and complacently wish them well . . . for they are our sons, our husbands, our fathers, our sweethearts; and it is our battle they are fighting."

Dr. Lowe cast the war as a spiritual struggle: "Life without God, life without truth, life without justice, would be mere existence. These values are worth preserving; and since they are worth preserving, they are worth defending." In April 1943 he lent his oratorical skills to the forty-eight-million-dollar war bond drive in Minneapolis and Hennepin County: "In this war, every rivet, every shoe, every shell, every helmet is of vital significance. Without them, our men are useless and our ideals are vapor. Do you not see and sense the terrific responsibility which confronts us?"

>>>

After training at Quantico, Virginia, Corporal Ralph Becker's platoon in the Third Marine Division moved to an undisclosed location in the South Pacific—a "beautiful island nearly half way around the world" (probably Guam)—and awaited orders to invade Japan. In this undated letter, probably written in late 1943, he thanks Dr. Lowe for sending him a New Testament: "I shall carry it with me wherever I go."

1941	December 1941	April 1942	February 1943
Fort Snelling begins training 300,000 soldiers for war	Japanese bomb the U.S. Pacific fleet in Pearl Harbor, bringing the United States into the war	U.S. troops stationed in the Philippines surrender to Japan	Germans surrender at Stalingrad in the first big defeat of Hitler's armies

celebrations, and plans for General Assembly's Minneapolis meeting in 1945. Often he sent copies of his sermons, church bulletins, and books: a New Testament or a light mystery. To Edwin Elwell, who lectured on malaria prevention, he mailed *The Case of the Drowsy Mosquito.*

If his letters seem facile or insensitive today, servicemen's and servicewomen's responses suggest otherwise. They wrote dozens of letters back. George Flannery thanked Lowe for Walter Lippman's *U.S. War Aims* and sent a full review from India. Dorothy Otterson, a Red Cross worker in Italy, shared details of her romance with an American flier lost for months in Rumania. "I wish everyone knew how important it is . . . to write cheerfully and chattily and frequently . . . to always make the boy feel as though he is being missed constantly," Anne Winslow wrote from the San Antonio Aviation Cadet Center.

When a soldier's faith wavered, Lowe was reassuring: "In a world such as this, it is not easy to lay hold on God. And yet, it is good to remember that doubts need not be sources of despair. Doubts may become challenges to more consistent thinking and to a more substantial philosophy of life." Every evening, he told them, he and his wife read over the entire list of Westminster men and women in service to "introduce them into our quiet hour of prayer."

For all his patriotism, Lowe did not bear grudges against America's opponents. In 1949 he traveled to Germany to survey the rubble. When he returned, he championed the cause of rebuilding the Reformierte Gemeinde, a Presbyterian church in Frankfurt. ✛

>>>

His deep sympathy for young men and women on the battlefield was kindled by his own service in World War I as an enlisted man in the 149th Machine Gun Battalion of the 42nd or Rainbow Division. "It was through this experience that I became wholly identified with this country and its people," he later wrote. "The sense of divided loyalty had gone." In the summer of 1918 he had seen heavy action in Château-Thierry, Ourque, and the Argonne. After the war his unit had moved through Trier, Coblenz, Bonn, and Cologne, much the same territory traversed by U.S. troops in 1944-45. "I know every house and every room in that town," he wrote to a soldier in Andernach.

Dr. Lowe filled his letters with chatty details about life in Minnesota: the nasty weather, the Gophers' dismal record, and the opening of pheasant season. He relayed stories of church events, Easter

June 1943	June 1944	May 1945	1947
Liquidation of all Jewish ghettos in Poland	Allies invade Normandy, France, on D-Day	Germany surrenders unconditionally	Nearly half of Minnesota's college and university students are WWII veterans attending under G.I. Bill

UNITED STATES ARMY AIR FORCES
SCOTT FIELD ILLINOIS

3505 AAFBU
Squadron P, Bks. 146
Scott Field, Illinois
16 February 1945

Dear Dr. Lowe,

Thanks a lot for the autographed copy of "You, the Jury"
which you sent me for Christmas. It arrived here at
Scott Field about a week ago. It had quite a struggle
catching up with me, and made two trips across the
Atlantic and two across the United States before it
finally made it. I thought the book was a particularly
good mystery story. It is now making the rounds of the
barracks and the other fellows send thanks also.

I have been to Santa Ana, California since I was home
on furlough and after being thoroughly tested, examined,
processed, inspected, and passed as serviceable, I was
sent to this base for refresher work in radio.
What assignment I will get after I finish here, I have
not the slightest way of knowing.

I was sorry to have to pass up your kind invitation for
lunch, but, as you may know already, my brother arrived
in Chicago several days before I was due to leave on
my trip back to the Army. My parents and I jumped on
the train and we were able to get our family together
for a brief two day visit for the first time since
February 1942. This meant that I missed out on some
of the things I had intended to do in Minneapolis.
Bob followed me to the West Coast a little later and
is now training for sea duty. After he leaves the
States he will be participating in action of the type
that took place over Tokyo last night.

Thanks again for your Christmas gift as well as for
the letters and Westminster News that I have been
getting through the past years.

Sincerely,

Bill Braddock

Dr. Lowe's letters and packages traveled the globe, sometimes
more than once, in search of their recipients. In a letter penned in
February 1945 Bill Braddock thanks Dr. Lowe for a mystery book,
which "made two trips across the Atlantic" before reaching him in
Illinois, where Braddock was training as a radio specialist.

*"No man who does not know how to be quiet can
be strong. He can only be loud and he can only be
busy . . . . We have come to act as though there were
something particularly redeeming about being busy.
We don't have time to pray."*

Arnold Lowe, talk at the YWCA, October 1964

Many servicemen and servicewomen exchanged Christmas greetings
with Dr. Lowe. Jim Van Valkenburg, a member of the 386th Infantry
Regiment, took a break from practicing amphibious landings at Camp
San Luis Obispo in 1944 to write this note on his first Christmas away
from home.

Music Directors

Harry Phillips *(1901-1924)*

Rupert Sircom *(1930-1962)*

Edward Berryman *(1962-1987)*

Peter Hendrickson *(1989-1994)*

Stephen Sheftz *(1994-1999)*

Melanie Ohnstad
*(Organist, 1995-present;
Minister of Music & Arts,
2000-present)*

The grandeur of the music program in the Lowe era suited the formality of Westminster's worship. A congregational campaign in the mid-1920s had replaced the unreliable pneumatic organ with a state-of-the art Kimball known as a "romantic" organ. With forty-nine stops and 3,582 pipes, it occupied a "thermostatically regulated" space the size of seven modest rooms. When a new Moeller organ was installed in the 1980s, a few ranks of the Kimball were retained. The current Minister of Music and the Arts, Melanie Ohnstad, calls them "among the finest sounds in the organ."

A stellar organ required a master organist. Rupert Sircom, a young virtuoso trained out East, was hired in 1930 and established himself as the consummate church organist and choir director by the 1940s. He filled every silence in the worship service with improvisation. Noted for his mastery of Bach, he offered organ recitals on weekday evenings. His dedication to impeccable music knew few boundaries. In the winter when the sanctuary went unheated during the week, he practiced in a tent constructed around the organ with a heater at his feet.

Under Sircom's direction, the choir became a highly disciplined unit in wine-colored robes, with the women sporting beanies and the men donning white shirts and uniform black neckties. He held the choir at precisely forty voices and expected absentees to find their own substitutes or be expelled. Vacancies were advertised and filled by competitive audition, and all positions were paid at least a token sum until the mid-1950s. The choir rehearsed twelve anthems in an hour and a half, and soloists practiced their parts separately. Sunday morning was often the first time the choir heard an anthem in full.

Sircom sought to educate the congregation as well. For as long as the weekly *Westminster* was published in the 1930s, it carried a column called "Music Notes" that introduced and discussed the choir anthems for the next Sunday. He expanded the repertoire in new directions, conducting the choir in the U.S. debut of Ralph Vaughn Williams's *Mass in g minor* in 1951.

Sircom's predecessor, Harry Phillips, had taken the choir beyond the worship context to offer public performances of European sacred music. Sircom arranged multi-choir concerts with invited singers. Bach's *The Passion According to St. Matthew* became a Palm Sunday tradition and involved all the choirs of the church,

including the many children's choirs that Sircom organized with the assistance of Gertrude Hognander. For the performance of the Passion on Palm Sunday 1962, Sircom directed a choir of 80 children and 110 adults, including the choir of the Cathedral of St. Mark.

It was the last concert of his life.

After the first service on Easter Sunday 1962, while the strains of Handel's "Hallelujah Chorus" echoed in the sanctuary, Sircom dismissed the choir to breakfast, then collapsed from a heart attack. He died en route to the hospital. A valiant substitute, Betty Lynch, stepped in, and the choir, as alto Lola Barnes remembers, "limped along." News of Sircom's death was withheld until the end of the second service.

Sircom was already set to retire, and his replacement, Edward Berryman, had been selected. Berryman was an even more skillful organist with a vast amount of music committed to memory. He opened the choir to members of the congregation with good voices who lacked professional training, but he still kept a high standard. Berryman continued the performance tradition and set up concert series that featured instrumentalists as well. Worship services on Passion Sunday and the third Sunday in Advent were devoted to oratorios or other major works of music. The children's choirs flourished, with the able assistance of Berryman's wife, Gladys. The sight of the children marching in on festival Sundays, with epaulets on the sleeves of their surplices marking their years in the choir, is a fond memory from the 1960s-70s. ✝

At left: The choir ca. 1935. The gentleman standing in the center of the front row is Rupert Sircom. His wife, soprano Mildred Sircom, stands to his right.

At right: Edward Berryman rehearses the adult choir and the children's choir.

CHALLENGE AND RESPONSE

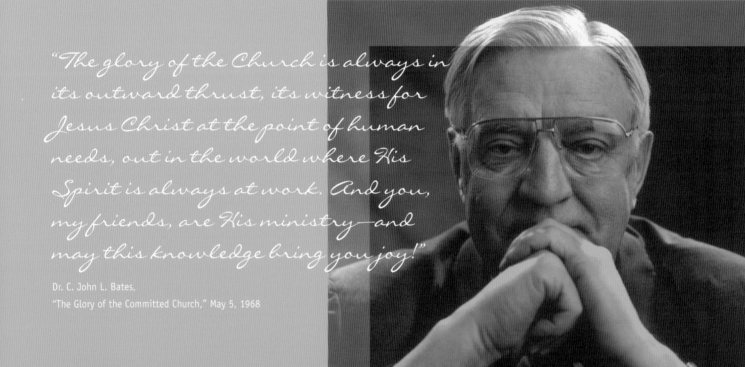

"The glory of the Church is always in its outward thrust, its witness for Jesus Christ at the point of human needs, out in the world where His Spirit is always at work. And you, my friends, are His ministry—and may this knowledge bring you joy!"

Dr. C. John L. Bates,
"The Glory of the Committed Church," May 5, 1968

Former Senator and Vice President of the United States Walter Mondale, a Westminster layman, exemplifies a faithful commitment to Christ's work in the world.

RACE AND OUR NEW RESPONSIBILITY

On a February evening in 1956 the Westminster Mothers Club gathered at the home of Mrs. William (Ellen) McCabe to hear a speaker from the Joint Committee for Equal Opportunity. This is the first documented instance of Westminster members responding to the issues of race that the bus boycott underway in Montgomery, Alabama, brought to public awareness. Two years earlier the U.S. Supreme Court laid the legal foundation for desegregation in Brown v. Board of Education. The boycotters found moral justification in Exodus and the Gospels.

That same February week Session responded testily to a query from General Assembly about the church's racial policies, declaring "emphatically that Westminster Church has been a so-called integrated church for many years and has practiced interracial fellowship within its membership throughout its long history. The ministers and the Session of Westminster Church wish to declare furthermore that there are at the present time many members of different races within its communicant membership." There was

a significant minority of Chinese American members, and the church had been engaged with the Chinese community since 1880, but otherwise the portrait seems illusory. In fact doubts had surfaced about the separate status of the Chinese Sunday school.

The Mothers Club was far out ahead of the congregation. The Civil Rights movement caught Westminster with its gaze turned inward, like much of cold war American Christianity. Church happened on Sunday morning and, for the women, in weekly Bible study. Fellowship was keyed to age, gender, and marital status. Mission meant sending money abroad or to campus ministry. Ten more years passed before the Sunday bulletin routinely listed programs on race. Often phrased, "The Negro and . . . ," they featured >>>

Top right: Peace activists rally at the State Capitol on May 9, 1970, after marching from the University of Minnesota campus. The Vietnam War prompted many such marches and rallies.

Bottom right: Guest speakers Mr. and Mrs. Charles Johnson inaugurate a series of Sunday morning discussions begun by Westminster's Task Force on Race and Religion on July 14, 1968. Among the listeners are Jim *(left)* and Peggy Tillitt *(nearest the wall).*

At right: Loring Nicollet Center, founded by Plymouth Congregational Church in 1954, provided after-school activities for neighborhood children. Westminster's participation marked a return to hands-on mission after a hiatus. The Loring Nicollet-Bethlehem Community Centers, which provide an array of social services, still draw volunteers and funds from Westminster.

The Reverend C. John L. Bates

The Reverend Cornelius John Lighthall Bates, Jr., Westminster's pastor from 1965 to 1972, called himself an "ecumaniac." Raised in Japan and ordained in the United Church of Canada, he had a global sensibility that kept him receptive to new ideas and unfamiliar people. Dr. Bates helped open the joint Thanksgiving service to Catholics and Jews, assisted a Catholic priest in a wedding in Westminster's chapel, and officiated at the first sanctuary baptism on record of the child of a single mother. He led Westminster through a time of significant and often discomfiting change in American society, and his poetry and comic wit eased his congregants' passage. It is fitting that Dr. Bates was the pastor when Westminster hosted General Assembly in that turbulent year, 1968.

>>>

local spokespeople like Lillian Anthony and Theatrice Williams, likely over-booked by church groups examining race at a safe distance on familiar turf.

The wider church offered leadership on urgent issues. The bulletin of September 22, 1963, two months before President Kennedy's assassination, carried a top-of-the-page appeal from Presbytery for letters to Congress in support of the Civil Rights bill. Dr. Lowe had already telegrammed Senators McCarthy and Humphrey and Congressman Fraser. Westminster Fellowship, a nation-wide youth group, began a study of prejudice, and seven of our youth attended an interfaith, interracial retreat in 1965.

The PCUSA's proposed Confession of 1967 called for "a present witness to God's grace" with bearing on contemporary social issues. This notion incited some conservative Presbyterians to form the opposition Lay Committee, still active in 2007 on ordination and sexuality. In the wary middle ground, where much of Westminster's congregation sat, concern about blurring the lines between God and Caesar governed decisions. Session, for example, denied

1961	1962	1963	1963
Peace Corps founded	Cuban Missile Crisis	Martin Luther King, Jr. delivers his "I Have a Dream" speech	John F. Kennedy assassinated in Dallas
	Rachel Carson publishes *Silent Spring*		

use of the sanctuary in 1967 for a speech by the theologian Robert McAfee Brown on grounds that it was political rather than religious. (Fourteen years later a thousand people came to hear Dr. Brown at the Town Hall Forum.)

Dr. Lowe retired in 1965. His successor, the Reverend C. John L. Bates, brought a new vision of the church's relationship to social change. A statement in the October 16, 1966, bulletin affirmed Westminster's strength as "a vital center of Christian witness," and then continued, "To keep its life, Westminster must also serve the society in which it lives. What we do here reaches into the innermost problems of our own city, the communities that surround it, and the world beyond it. The extent to which we of Westminster become involved will prove the measure of our effective witness to Christ. This is our new responsibility." Dr. Bates elaborated on this message at the 1967 congregational meeting, distinguishing between "the church gathered and the church in dispersion," at work outside its walls.

Peggy Tillitt remembers the late 1960s as "a very exciting time to be a member and to be involved, because we had not initiated any new mission projects in recent years." She credits Associate Pastor Thomas Zemek, called in September 1966, with urging Westminster into the community. "He and Dr. Bates took some turns that took us right outside our doors." Zemek was raised in Chicago, home to a large black population whose forebears had come up from the Mississippi Delta in the Great Migration after World War I. He had marched from Selma to Montgomery, Alabama, in 1965 and met Twin Citians there. The Zemeks were among the first families to adopt interracially, so race was of intimate concern.

Minneapolis had a small black community, some of whose ancestors had arrived before statehood. Now African Americans fleeing poverty in other cities had settled on the Near Northside, the old Hope Chapel neighborhood, vacated by suburb-bound children of Jewish immigrants. The prospect of an "inner city" in orderly Minneapolis frightened many white people, and their fears seemed realized in August 1966 and July 1967 when rioting >>>

"To keep its life, Westminster must also serve the society in which it lives. What we do here reaches into the innermost problems of our own city, the communities that surround it, and the world beyond it. The extent to which we of Westminster become involved will prove the measure of our effective witness to Christ. This is our new responsibility."

Representatives from the church and the community, including Peggy Tillitt, Ellen McCabe, and Rev. Tom Zemek, discuss the Day Activity Center for mentally disabled teenagers housed at Westminster from 1967-71.

1964	1965	1968	1968	1970
Civil Rights Act outlaws discrimination based on race, color, religion, sex, or national origin	Malcolm X assassinated

U.S. troops sent to Vietnam | Martin Luther King, Jr. assassinated in Memphis

Tet offensive | Shirley Chisholm elected America's first black Congresswoman | Kent State student demonstrators killed by National Guard troops |

Dr. Martin Luther King, Jr. speaks against the War in Vietnam on the St. Paul campus of the University of Minnesota, April 27, 1967.

>>>

damaged businesses along Plymouth Avenue. Tom Zemek, who had established ties in the community, rallied Westminster members to join a March of Support down Plymouth Avenue after the assassination of Dr. Martin Luther King, Jr. in April 1968. "John Bates took a deep breath," Peggy Tillitt recalls. "This wasn't something Westminster would usually do."

At the next Session meeting the Clerk read a letter from a group of members requesting a committee on religion and race. The task force appointed consisted largely of married couples. Their first achievement was sending boys from Dayton Avenue Church in St. Paul to Camp Ajawah. Their major effort was "self-education," a deeper study of the issues that would inform action in the community. An attempt to call a black pastor to conduct a street

ministry failed at the Presbytery level. By 1972 the Task Force on Religion and Race, renamed Church and Society, had become a standing committee of Session with purview over all social issues.

Westminster again took a serious look at race with the Vision 2000 long-range plan. A Task Team on Racism and Diversity was constituted in 1997 "to work as a community of faith to combat individual and institutional racism and prejudice and to celebrate and promote diversity in the life of Westminster Presbyterian Church." Once again an associate pastor with experience in bridging cultures is charged with taking us out the door from education to action. The Reverend Douglas Mitchell came of age in Birmingham, Alabama, in those turbulent 1960s. ✛

Boiler room ministry AL COOPER

At right: Al and Sharon Cooper.

Below left: Al *(seated)* in his boiler room office with custodian Ted Van Kempen, 1969.

Late in the last century when Westminster's coffee service went all decaf for a time, rumors floated that a real jolt of caffeine might be found in the boiler room. Strong coffee was not the most vital nourishment that Facilities Manager Alvan Cooper served up in his thirty-six and a half years on staff. Conversation, counsel, practical help, and a Good Samaritan kindness were available to all comers, from troubled deacons to curious teenagers to intoxicated transients. "My door was open to anybody," Cooper remembers.

Ushers ducked out on the sermon and headed for the boiler room for coffee and conversation that could be light-hearted or serious. Teenagers, including those Cooper caught riding the dumb waiter down into the locked kitchen, dropped in for counsel about family problems or sex or drinking. He counts some of them among his current adult friends. Although Cooper is retired, he's still "open" as a reception desk volunteer.

Al Cooper knows many of the homeless people downtown by name. His approach is simple: "You know, if you treat them with respect, you get nothing but respect back again." He outfitted many with jackets and gloves and shoes from a supply in the boiler

room locker. "The Clothes Closet on Central was only open on Tuesdays and Thursdays, and these guys were freezing on Saturday." He handed out money, against church policy. "If you give me a story that I'll buy or that I haven't used myself, then you got it." Sometimes respect means straight talk. Cooper can call a bluff as only one who has been chemically dependent himself can. "I never asked to be reimbursed," he says, "because I'm offering something that was given to me a long time ago." He credits Associate Pastor Tom Zemek for helping him get his life in order.

"He told me that this place will get to you, which it did. He said when you walk out the door you become a symbol of Westminster Church no matter where you go, if you have a uniform on or not. And all of a sudden that's the way I lived."

Westminster changed Cooper's life in another major way. He met his wife, Sharon, now the Office Manager, who practices her own pastoral ministry on the second floor, listening compassionately to parishioners who call or drop by, especially those in grief. As clergy have come and gone since 1968, Al and Sharon have been mainstays of the church's daily life.

One day a man Cooper had driven to detox months before stopped him on the street and asked if he could still come by the church and talk now that he was sober. As they were parting, the man, a Native American, remarked, "You cast a big shadow." As Cooper would say about everything he appreciates at Westminster, that's the magic of this place.

His boiler room ministry didn't diminish the quality of Cooper's assigned work. Director of Administration Sam Cooke attributes the success of the sanctuary renovation and the Marquette addition to Al Cooper's respectful inch-by-inch knowledge of the church building. ✛

High into the blue

FAITH NIXON AND WOMEN'S MINISTRIES

1972 was a year of irrevocable change for the women of Westminster. Three more female elders had joined the first two elected in 1970, and four women had just become deacons. Barbara Freeman and Mary Lee Dayton sat on the Board of Trustees. It was time to let go of the final remnant of the church's segregated past, the Women's Association, which had maintained a separate program, governance structure, and budget since the Sewing Society began in 1859. While they welcomed access to the core leadership of the church, many women felt wary of losing the autonomy, vitality, and fellowship they had enjoyed in their separate sphere. An article in *Westminster News* announcing the schedule of Westminster on Wednesday, traditionally women's day at church, spoke to this fear. Invoking the pop culture figure Jonathan Livingston Seagull, it urged, "No staying around the familiar fishing boats and diving for scraps of food and bread. We're going to soar high into the blue and explore the horizons."

The article's author, Faith Nixon, was never one to hang around the boat, but neither would she abandon the timid birds and soar off alone. Throughout her nearly sixty years at Westminster, she set the pace for the flock.

Faith Thies came to Westminster on her own as a teenager for the timely, stimulating programs of the Tuxis Society. She joined the church as a communicant in 1932. Herman Sweet, Director of Religious Education, challenged the youth and young adults to apply their faith to serious public issues. Dr. Boddy's assistant, Edith Cochrane, helped lead their lively discussions. Thies also participated in church drama groups as actress and director. Conservative members of Session disapproved of these "secular" programs and tried to veto some that the youth themselves had planned. In a coup unusual for Westminster, the youth enlisted Dr. Boddy's help in appointing an "unofficial" nominating committee that was then voted into legitimacy at the 1934 congregational meeting. It added three seats to the Session and filled them with younger men sympathetic to the youth. Faith Thies was later elected secretary of the Young People's Cabinet. Norman Nixon served on its executive committee.

Faith and Norman were married on June 12, 1937, and moved on to education and fellowship for married couples. Norman was elected to the Board of Deacons in 1941 and ordained as an elder in 1966. Faith gave her energy to the women's work.

She was president of the Women's Association in 1960 when it underwent a stressful reorganization to accord with the United Presbyterian Women's National Plan. The venerable but declining Helen Daniels Guild, founded in 1925, and its younger sister, the Priscilla Circle, were dissolved and replaced with nine circles not defined by age or marital status. Dr. Lowe opposed the change, but Nixon saw benefits in a stronger relationship with women of the broader church.

At the congregational meeting on January 23, 1969, Clerk of Session Andrew Hobart moved that the Nominating Committee be "specially urged" to consider women for the church boards next time around. >>>

Above: Faith Nixon was a generous and candid mentor to younger women, including Cheri Register, shown here in 1983 with her daughters, Maria and Grace De Jong.

Edith Prideaux Cochrane came to Westminster in 1934 as the assistant to the pastor under Dr. Boddy. She joined the congregation and served the church with gentle, persistent lay leadership until her death in 1990. Of keen intellect and radiant spirit, she was one of the first two women elected elder in 1970, along with Helen Woodhull Kramer. Cochrane chaired the committee that wrote *A Telling Presence*, Westminster's 1982 history book.

>>>

The motion passed with only "a brief comment," perhaps an explanation that the office of elder had been open to women since 1930. House of Hope in St. Paul had been electing women since 1956. Faith Nixon and Caroline Ewe were the only women on the Nominating Committee that year. They may well deserve credit for the choice of two exemplary candidates, Edith Cochrane and Helen Kramer. Nixon herself was elected in 1973.

Nixon was an engaged and vocal member of Session. With the Clerk of Session absent, the Reverend Donald Meisel appointed her clerk pro tem for the November 8, 1973, meeting. Hers is the first female signature in 116 years of Session minutes. This honor hardly assured compliant behavior. Nixon believed that communion ought to be a joyful feast. Dr. Meisel wanted it solemn and dignified.

> *Reminded yet again about appropriate dress, she announced to the Session, "I never wear black and I always look dignified." Out in the narthex between the passing of bread and wine, Nixon, cheery in her plum or lilac suit, would gesture toward a group of male elders and whisper, "They look like a bunch of pall bearers."*

When the Reverend Ellen Babinsky arrived in 1976 to become Westminster's first female minister, Faith Nixon was on staff as secretary to the assistant pastors. "She was a bright light with this wonderful smile," Rev. Babinsky recalls, "and you always knew >>>

1920
Motion to ordain women as elders narrowly fails to gain approval from a majority of presbyteries

1930
Female elders approved in the PCUSA

1944
Cedar Rapids Presbytery ordains Elizabeth Brinton Clark to the Ministry of Word and Sacrament; overruled by GA

1956
GA passes motion to ordain women as ministers of Word and Sacrament in the PCUSA

Three of Westminster's growing succession of female associate pastors: Rev. Anna Carter Florence (1988-93), Rev. Ellen Babinsky (1976-83), and Rev. Elizabeth Heller (1983-93, plus interim appointments).

Dr. Deborah Mullen, Dean of Masters Programs at McCormick Theological Seminary in Chicago, was one of several female clergy who preached at Westminster in summer 2006 to mark the fiftieth anniversary of the ordination of women to the Ministry of Word and Sacrament.

Two of our current associate pastors, Rev. Kathy Michael and Rev. Annika Lister Stroope, flank Rev. Susan Andrews, Moderator of the General Assembly, on Gifts of Women Sunday in 2004.

>>>

what she thought. Whether you wanted to know it or not, you always knew it. Whatever strengths I exhibited at Westminster, I have to say that I received an enormous amount of energy and strength from the women. Faith Nixon was emblematic of that kind of energy, forthrightness, and care."

Ten years after the Women's Association's demise, programs of interest to women were flourishing enough to warrant the Session's attention. Elder Elizabeth Heller had been ordained as clergy and hired on an interim basis. Women in the congregation sought opportunities for "their" two ministers to use their gifts fully.

Session added a Committee on Women's Ministries in 1982 and Faith Nixon, recently widowed, agreed to chair it. She championed weekend retreats and special women's worship services and spoke with enthusiasm about the new Anne Hutchinson Circle and its

programs on feminist theology. She was pleased that her beloved Westminster still attracted younger people with fresh ideas. When the Worship Committee took up the issue of inclusive language, Nixon brought a resolution to Session: "A basic assumption of the Women's Ministries Board is that language used in worship and work of the church should affirm the wholeness of God and full personhood of all." She had no personal quarrel with the familiar language, but if it made others feel excluded, then it ought to be changed.

Nixon passed away on August 18, 1988, after refusing aggressive treatment for cancer. Weeks before her death she told one of the younger women, "You girls are going to die when you see the hymns I've chosen for my funeral." They didn't die. They sang out "Dear Lord and Father of Mankind" in celebration of Faith Nixon's ability to look back with reverence while flying ever forward. ✛

1956
Margaret Towner becomes the first woman officially ordained by the PCUSA

1959
Miriam Ortega becomes the first woman ordained by the Presbytery of Cuba

CHALLENGE AND RESPONSE

Hymn 478 traditional

[Old lyrics] Henry Francis Lyte, 1834; alt.

Praise, my soul, the King of heaven; to His feet they tribute bring;

Ransomed, healed, restored, forgiven, Evermore His praises sing:

Alleluia! Alleluia! Praise the everlasting King.

Praise Him for His grace and favor To His people in distress;

Praise Him still the same as ever, Slow to chide, and swift to bless:

Alleluia! Alleluia! Glorious in His faithfulness.

Father-like He tends and spares us; Well our feeble frame He knows;

In His hands He gently bears us, Rescues us from all our foes.

Alleluia! Alleluia! Widely yet His mercy flows.

Angels, help us to adore Him: Ye behold Him face to face;

Sun and moon, bow down before Him, Dwellers all in time and space.

Alleluia! Alleluia! Praise with us the God of grace.

Hymn 479 inclusive language

[New lyrics] Adapted by the Ecumenical Women's Center, 1974

Praise, My soul, the God of heaven, Glad of heart your carols raise;

Ransomed, healed, restored, forgiven, Who, like me, should sing God's praise?

Alleluia! Alleluia! Praise the Maker all your days!

Praise God for the grace and favor Shown our forebears in distress;

God is still the same forever, Slow to chide and swift to bless.

Alleluia! Alleluia! Sing our Maker's faithfulness!

Like a loving parent caring, God knows well our feeble frame;

Gladly all our burdens bearing, Still to countless years the same.

Alleluia! Alleluia! All within me, praise God's name!

Angels, teach us adoration, You behold God face to face;

Sun and moon and all creation, Dwellers all in time and space.

Alleluia! Alleluia! Praise with us the God of grace!

Who is my neighbor? HMONG REFUGEES

Sundays at Westminster Vietnam veterans sit among aging anti-war activists and men whose spiritual training at Camp Ajawah won them conscientious objector status. Yet to judge from church documents of 1960-75, the Vietnam War left Westminster untouched, with one exception: Colonel David W. Winn, a member held for four years and seven months as a POW in Hanoi, addressed the first Open Forum on April 29, 1973, and returned as Brigadier General to preach a sermon on how faith sustained him.

When a young member asked in 1970 for guidance on the war, Session discussed "the appropriateness of such a statement" and "the increasing division among church members as to the application of Christian principles to this issue." Mention of the war was left to Rev. Bates's discretion. No names of Westminster servicemen and nurses were listed in the bulletin. No adult education on reconciling war with faith. No panels on Vietnam policy. No uniformed homecomings. No bronze tablet in the Cloister Hall like those listing world war veterans.

Yet the Vietnam War touches Westminster every Friday, when the rickety Boy Scout bus pulls up to unload Troop 100, new Hmong refugees and American-born sons of parents whose lives and culture the war upended. Few Minnesotans knew of the Hmong in 1981 when three hundred Asian teenagers appeared at Edison High School, where Westminster's Dave Moore taught social studies. "They were totally out of it, totally frightened, totally lost,"

he remembers. The Hmong had kept an intact cultural identity for centuries while farming in remote areas of China and Southeast Asia. When the Plain of Jars in the Highlands of neutral Laos became strategically important to the United States, the Central Intelligence Agency recruited the Hmong to fight in a "Secret War." The end of the war exposed them to the vengeance of the Pathet Lao. Hmong families swam the Mekong River into Thailand, to refugee camps where some still wait for asylum abroad.

Moore taught the students scouting skills by miming knots and games. "The kids caught on and they just loved it, so they wanted to keep doing it." Westminster's Troop 33 would have welcomed the boys, but Moore thought they needed a transitional space respectful of Hmong culture, so Troop 100 was created. Several Westminster women taught English to Hmong adults, and church funding launched a Hmong American scholarship. A Girl Scout troop was attempted, but parents were reluctant to let their daughters venture far from home.

The rate at which Troop 100 produced Eagle Scouts astonished its Presbyterian sponsors. Eagle Scout Cy Thao, now in the Minnesota House of Representatives, explains, "I think Boy Scouts came naturally to a lot of us because when we were in the refugee camps we were always outdoors. And in daily life in the camp, you have to cook on an open fire and go fetch water. It's almost like the kids from the camps had been camping their whole lives." Some of the first scouts had even been soldiers in the Secret War.

At left: Eloise Giannobile with a family from Vietnam that she and her husband, Ted, sponsored in the 1970s. The Giannobiles and Ken and Diane Brinkman sought to interest Westminster's congregation in refugee sponsorship.

At right: Boys of Troop 100 are joined by their parents in a ceremony in Westminster's chapel promoting them to the rank of Eagle Scout.

Below: The artist and Minnesota State Representative Cy Thao, whose paintings mimic the style of Hmong story tapestries, painted this reminiscence of Troops 100 and 33 boarding the Boy Scout bus in the old corner parking lot. Now part of Westminster's art collection, it was exhibited in the Westminster Gallery along with other works by Cy Thao in 2006.

Westminster never sought to convert the Hmong. "We try to make Camp Ajawah a Christian camp," Moore explains, "in the sense of living the Christian life." Cy Thao thinks back to Moore's practice of giving the best equipment to the youngest campers when he pursues legislation to aid the neediest Minnesotans. Leadership and loyalty are values that hold.

> *"A lot of the guys who went through Troop 100, who went far in the ranks or stayed a long time, today are some of the movers and shakers within the Hmong community. We're still carrying on the daily work of trying to do something better for the community."*

Cultural influence works both ways. As *Seng Sue Moua,* "Teacher," Dave Moore has attended family rituals, visited refugee camps in Thailand, and driven Scouts to college. Joint activities bring Troops 33 and 100 together. "It was a big deal for me to have some friends outside of the Hmong community," Cy Thao attests. "I think a lot of the Hmong scouts who came through that troop tended to be more open, more willing to get to know someone outside their own community, to get out of their comfort zone." Nudging Westminster out of its comfort zone, including its silence about the Vietnam War, may be the legacy the Hmong offer. ✛

The Open Door OUTREACH WITHIN THE WALLS

The mid-1980s were contentious yet constructive years at Westminster: contentious because of new challenges to the church's understanding of mission; constructive because a capital campaign allowed for remodeling of the parish house. The campaign stirred contention about the ratio of mission giving to money spent on facilities.

The country had taken a conservative turn with Ronald Reagan's election in 1980, away from the New Deal legacy of social welfare. Some churches stepped in to address homelessness and hunger as matters of social justice. St. Stephen's Catholic Church south of downtown opened a homeless shelter in 1982 and began serving free meals, called "Loaves and Fishes." Westminster members volunteered there and at the Groveland Food Shelf at Plymouth Congregational Church, but our church had not housed a mission program since the Day Activity Center for mentally disabled teens in the 1960s. Following St. Stephen's example would seem a radical departure for Westminster.

In 1982 St. Luke's Presbyterian Church in Wayzata offered sanctuary, safety inside sacred space, to a Salvadoran refugee seeking asylum in the United States. A multi-denominational Sanctuary movement helped people whose lives were at risk escape political violence in El Salvador and Guatemala by housing them in churches and providing legal advocacy. St. Luke's asked Westminster for moral and practical support and to consider offering sanctuary. Clerk Art Nelson's request that all elders "have a Christian outlook toward the question" didn't produce consensus. Disputed reports that the United States secretly fueled the civil wars turned the Sanctuary movement into a partisan matter. While a majority of the Session welcomed the educational efforts of John and Maxine Sinclair, former missionaries in Latin America, and Duane Krohnke, a lawyer for the American Lutheran Church, discussion nevertheless reverted to the propriety of involving the church in politics. Cold war anxiety about Communism underlay some of the objections. Even Church and Society Chair Phyllis Sutton's cautiously crafted motions simply to inform the congregation about channels for individual support encountered vigorous opposition before passing. (Rene Hurtado, St. Luke's guest, finally won clearance to stay in the U.S. in January 2007.)

The remodeled building, with new offices and dining room, refurbished meeting rooms named for pastors, an elevator, and the Lowe Library was feted on Dedication/Rededication Sunday, April 21, 1985. The next annual meeting took place January 26, 1986. Expected to be a pro forma election of officers, it became a dramatic moment-of-truth. On the call for new business, Deacon Roger Woo stood and spoke with a quiet urgency. He would like to see us open our beautiful building to our homeless and hungry neighbors, but he sensed that Westminster was more concerned with the condition of its physical plant than with human need. He was sorry that we hadn't participated in the Sanctuary movement.

Woo was a familiar figure who usually observed events through a camera lens as Westminster's photographer. Few knew of his long personal mission with the city's American Indian community, nor did the congregation's collective memory extend back to the 1880s, when Woo's grandfather and great uncle, Chinese immigrants scorned as aliens, found a welcome at Westminster. >>>

Above: The Open Door logo was designed by member Gordon Schlichting in 1979 and has been modified three times since.

Roger Woo visits with Mary Day, a longtime teacher in the Chinese Sunday School, 1967.

On the call for new business, Deacon Roger Woo stood and spoke with a quiet urgency. He would like to see us open our beautiful building to our homeless and hungry neighbors, but he sensed that Westminster was more concerned with the condition of its physical plant than with human need. He was sorry that we hadn't participated in the Sanctuary movement.

>>>

Five months later Roger Woo was dead of cancer at fifty-seven, but his jolt to Westminster's conscience outlived him. The Mission Committee created a task force to consider "an on-going hands-on ministry within the walls of Westminster." At the 1987 congregational meeting the task force proposed two programs to be sponsored by the Deacons: a gathering one Saturday a month to offer "support and nutrition to frail and poor elderly people," and a Sunday meal once a month to supplement the week-night Loaves and Fishes program at St. Stephen's. To win endorsement from the congregation, Dr. Meisel invoked the memory of Roger Woo.

The program that became Saturday Friends was well received, but the meal that became F.E.A.S.T. (Friends Eating and Sharing Together) remained in contention. At its March meeting Session discussed whether the clientele would threaten the integrity and security of the building. A motion to approve a three- to six-month trial was submitted to a secret ballot and passed sixteen to five. After the meal's first run in May the Deacons reported, "None of the apprehensions that had been anticipated were realized."

Saturday Friends was discontinued in 2004 after attendance declined. Two other in-house programs that date from the 1980s have benefited Westminster's outreach efforts: the Counseling Center and the Town Hall Forum. Roger Woo's plea lives on, here in Faith in Action Council Co-Chair Gretchen Musicant's words,

"Sure we have F.E.A.S.T. once a month, but I think this beautiful place should be something that more people in the community feel is a resource for them. And I don't mean people just having more nice, orderly meetings here. It still feels a little bit too much ours and not enough the community's." ✛

THE COUNSELING CENTER

The Westminster Counseling Center traces its origins to collegial conversations in the 1970s between Associate Pastor George Easley and Dr. John Heefner, a psychiatrist and Westminster elder. Some concerns that Easley heard in pastoral visits needed ongoing therapeutic attention that none of the pastors felt equipped to provide. By 1976 the church's long-range plan called for a counseling center, and it opened in February 1979. Several counselors and health professionals from the congregation volunteered their services to parishioners referred by the pastors. The specter of legal liability reared up in 1986, and the church joined with Abbott Northwestern Hospital to establish an accredited program that was expected to sustain itself financially. It didn't, and the debts mounted.

The current model was created in the 1990s with the leadership of the Reverend Max Maguire, the hospital's longtime chaplain, who worships at Westminster. As chair of the Counseling Committee, David Koehler helped reconceive the Center as an outreach program. It is open to people of all faiths or no faith. The counselors, all with credentials in mental health care and theology, use religious language only if the client invites it. A generous sliding-fee scale makes quality psychological care accessible to the poor and uninsured. As needed, clients are referred to John Heefner and other physician volunteers for medical consultations. Surveys over the years show that about three-fourths of the people using the center come in from outside the church.

Although this was never its primary mission, the Counseling Center plays a role in evangelism as well. Some clients come to see Westminster as their spiritual home. Recently, a new member who was asked why he chose to join Westminster credited the Counseling Center's director:

"Margaret McCray saved my life." ✦

Five people who have contributed to the vitality of the Counseling Center: David Koehler, Margaret McCray, John Heefner, Max Maguire, and Sam Cooke.

TOWARD SELF-SUFFICIENCY

Westminster's first onsite outreach program in the post-World War II years actually dates to September 1967, when weekday classes for developmentally disabled teenagers began at church in partnership with the Minnesota Association for Retarded Citizens, now known as ARC. The public schools made no provision for these children beyond the elementary years, so MARC tried to fill the gap with Day Activity Centers. Transportation was an immediate need. Westminster volunteers met students at their homes, walked them to their bus stops, helped them board the correct bus, then jumped into their own cars and raced downtown to meet their charges and direct them to the church. After enough repetitions, the teens flew solo. Practical training in, for example, hygiene, laundry, money, and housekeeping also aimed toward self-sufficiency. By 1971 the public schools began their own classes, and Westminster's energy turned to the Community Involvement Program, a new non-profit that assisted developmentally disabled adults toward the same goal. Westminster first helped fund and furnish apartments where residents learned to live independently, with staff support in the building. CIP has grown, formed new partnerships, and extended its reach, but many Westminster members remain loyal as board members, donors, and volunteers. ✛

Unfortunately, there are no "after" photos in the church archives to show whether all the girls learning hair care at the Day Activity Center ended up with beehives.

F.E.A.S.T.

Westminster opened its refectory to about 150 walk-in dinner guests on May 24, 1987. Those who could be accommodated at tables sat down while others waited their turn. A cadre of volunteers divided the serving tasks: dishing up plates from a serving line, ferrying them to the tables, or pouring beverages. The scene has been repeated every fourth Sunday of the month for twenty years. The numbers fluctuate, at times toward four hundred. Men outnumber women, but economic downturns raise the number of families with children.

John Goepferd headed the cooking team until his recent retirement. He kept the meals simple: usually turkey or ham as the entrée. Tim Scott, a professional chef, has dressed the menu up a bit. The intent has always been to treat the diners as guests in one's own home. A pianist accompanies the meal, and books, magazines, and toiletries are available. Every child gets a book to keep. In the winter guests are welcome to outerwear collected at the church.

"It's not just a feeding program," Goepferd explains. "It's also a fellowship and a social program for a lot of people. We do see a lot of return visitors, on a monthly basis, who we've seen for years. It's not just for the homeless. It's also for people on fixed incomes, and their dollars just don't stretch as far as they used to." Isabel Goepferd adds, "In fact we also have several volunteers who are one step removed from being homeless. They appreciate the program so much, they come and help every month, and know that we can guarantee that they will get a good hot meal in return."

Asked how the program might grow, John says, "There definitely is a housing need. It's a matter of if we have space, if we want to take care of the space, if we want to have staff to do it. It is a big commitment to be able to do something like that." Isabel asks, "Ideally, wouldn't you like to think that we wouldn't need to have a program like F.E.A.S.T.?" ✤

Left: Gordon Hermanson at work in the kitchen. *Middle:* Erin Cochrane, Grace Kenney, Saskia Van Riessen, and Sarah Nealon, fourth graders in 2004-05, with winter scarves that they made in Sunday school for the F.E.A.S.T. guests. *Right:* Gretchen Musicant, Barbara Randolph-Anderson, Lucy Donaldson, and Lee Furman prepare to serve the meal.

THE REVEREND DONALD MEISEL

The Reverend Donald Morrison Meisel assumed Westminster's pulpit in October 1972 as a native son come home. A graduate of St. Paul Central High School and Macalester College, he earned degrees at Princeton Seminary and the University of Edinburgh and served three pastorates in New Jersey, including twelve years at the historic First Presbyterian Church in Princeton.

Worshipers hung on Dr. Meisel's intelligent and elegantly crafted sermons, which closed with a provocative twist not easily ignored. "His sermons always tenderized me," D'Arlyn Marks says. "They brought me up short and made me search myself." He delivered them in a resonant bass baritone softened with gentle wit, which a recent fifth grade Sunday school class employed as the voice of God in a video production.

A generational rift not solely determined by age marked Dr. Meisel's keenly attentive congregation. Some parishioners found solace in Arnold Lowe's legacy of formal worship and sturdy clerical authority and preferred to keep the church free of secular struggles. Others, nurtured in faith by the democratic social movements of the mid-century, sought engagement with the world. Like John Bushnell before him, Meisel carefully negotiated the middle ground.

Yet he certainly didn't cower when the world pressed in and demanded attention. During the Watergate hearings in 1973 he found a reference to Jerusalem's Water Gate in Nehemiah 8:1 and drew a bold parallel: "Our own Watergate represents an enslavement in our own land to avarice, suspicion, blind loyalty, confusion about ends and appropriate means of achieving them, lawlessness, hiding behind privilege, evasion, reluctant and inadequate coming to terms. How do we break out of it? Not, certainly, by developing or acquiescing in a religion which indiscriminately puts an equal sign between patriotism and faith . . . but by cultivating and serving a sense of God's transcendence, God's awe-full caring."

At an officers' retreat held to compose a mission statement for Westminster in 1977, Dr. Meisel suggested and argued for the phrase "a telling presence in the city," which quickly became a church motto. He forged relationships with city officials and downtown clergy behind the scenes and became a public voice for ethical leadership as moderator of the Town Hall Forum. In fact, his voice carries a long way. A stranger who overheard him talking along Lake Superior turned and greeted him by name.

One important legacy of Dr. Meisel's tenure was unintended. His wife, Eleanor, contracted a life-threatening cancer, the treatment for which disfigured her face. Without ever glossing over the reality of suffering, the Meisels modeled dignity and grace in adversity. Ellie Meisel wrote in the *Westminster News* that she preferred children's honest stares and questions to the fleeting glances adults thought she didn't see. Her forthrightness and good humor endeared her to the congregation.

Dr. Meisel retired in 1992 but continues to worship at Westminster and participate in its community as Pastor Emeritus. ✦

Voices of conscience: key issues in ethical perspective

THE TOWN HALL FORUM

At left: Anglican Archbishop Desmond Tutu of South Africa, anti-apartheid campaigner and head of the post-apartheid Truth and Reconciliation Commission, addressed the Town Hall Forum in February 1999. He was awarded the Nobel Peace Prize in 1984 as well as the Gandhi Peace Prize and many others.

At right: Paul and Diane Neimann, originators of the Town Hall Forum, visit with Lord Harold Wilson, former Prime Minister of the United Kingdom, who spoke at the Forum in 1985.

Mention Westminster in casual conversation and you will likely hear, Oh, that's the church that does the Town Hall Forum. The Forum was born over dinner at the manse on Lake Harriet one evening in fall 1979. "If it weren't for Paul and Diane Neimann, the Town Hall Forum wouldn't have happened," Dr. Meisel maintains. They were describing a public forum they had enjoyed while living in Pittsburgh and wondered whether such a thing might suit Westminster. Meisel, always alert to new ways to fulfill the church's mission as "a telling presence in the city," was intrigued. He and Diane discussed the idea the following week and agreed on a simple noontime program with an overarching theme. Meisel came up with "Voices of Conscience: Key Issues in Ethical Perspective." Session approved the plan with the proviso that it not drain the church's budget.

Archibald Cox, who chaired Common Cause and had served as a special prosecutor in the Watergate investigations, opened the series September 18, 1980, with a speech on "Government, Politics and the Spirit of America." Twelve hundred people attended. The second speaker, syndicated columnist Ellen Goodman, drew a standing-room-only crowd. Since the intent was to offer free admission, and the speakers commanded high fees, the Forum budget soon

exceeded individual donors' goodwill. By 1985 when the Neimanns stepped down as coordinators, 70 percent of the funding came from foundations and corporations. The current director, Susan McKenna, began her tenure in 2005. Together with the board of directors led by Peter Meyer, she has broadened fundraising efforts and publicity, introduced moderated post-forum discussion groups, and invited the sanctuary audience to a public reception for nearly every speaker.

Minnesota Public Radio began broadcasting the Forum in September 1982. It currently reaches an estimated sixty thousand listeners via American Public Radio. Because of the focus on ethics, many of the speakers address systemic injustices and propose far-reaching solutions to the problems the church addresses in its Faith in Action ministry. The Forum has a hand in evangelism, as well, attracting members who seek, as Duane Krohnke did, "a church that is open to rational discussion in the context of religious belief." The Reverend Timothy Hart-Andersen sees the Forum as a secular counterpart to Sunday worship that makes Westminster "a place where ideas matter, where minds are open, and where the future is forged in a civil engagement over the questions of our day." >>>

A SAMPLING OF SPEAKERS, 1980-2007

Below, from top: Archbishop Desmond Tutu holds the attention of a standing-room-only crowd.

Poet and memoirist Maya Angelou spoke—and sang—to the Town Hall Forum in September 1984.

Edward Albee	George McGovern
Isabel Allende	Walter Mondale
Maya Angelou	Mira Nair
Joyce Brothers	Michael Oppenheimer
Frederick Buechner	Parker Palmer
Shirley Chisholm	Gordon Parks
Robert Coles	Mary Pipher
Archibald Cox	William Proxmire
Morris Dees	José Ramos-Horta
Joe Dowling	Theodore Roosevelt, IV
Marion Wright Edelman	Salman Rushdie
James Fallows	Dean Rusk
Martin Friedman	Daniel Schorr
Thomas Friedman	Attaliah Shabazz
David Gergen	Isaac Bashevis Singer
Peter Gomes	John Shelby Spong
Ellen Goodman	Amy Tan
Lani Guinier	Studs Terkel
Mark Hatfield	Nina Totenberg
Bernice Johnson Reagon	Desmond Tutu
Garrison Keillor	Jim Wallis
C. Everett Koop	Cornel West
Jonathan Kozol	Elie Wiesel
Harold Kushner	
Martin Marty	

The purloined Celtic cross is now firmly anchored at the front of the sanctuary, between the pulpit and the organ.

WHY THE OPEN DOOR IS LOCKED

Church documents tell us that the Trustees in September 1988 were "wrestling with the issue of security." Church lore tells us that the word "wrestling" is apt. Office Manager Sharon Cooper once had to fend off an inebriated man who leapt the counter to disarm her of her letter opener.

As a group of men from the church staff left for lunch one day back in the 1970s, someone alerted them about a man carrying a cross. It wasn't Jesus on His way to Calvary. Indeed, the sanctuary cross was missing. They took off in different directions by foot and by car. Jack Terry and Tom Zemek were pursuing the man down Nicollet Avenue when Lloyd Peitzman, a college wrestling champion, rounded the corner and pinned him to the ground. In the meantime, Ed Berryman and Steve Tsui had scooped up two familiar vases the man's accomplice dropped on the sidewalk. The police arrested the man and impounded the evidence. When Terry went to the police property room to claim the loot, he spotted an antique chair that had gone missing months before.

The hiring of security guards in "soft" uniforms in the 1980s proved both inefficient and irritating to members used to free rein in the church. The locked-door security system and the open door logo are, ironically, about the same age. Of course anyone with a suitable reason for entering the church is cheerfully buzzed in, and scores of Boy Scouts have memorized the keypad code. ✛

HOW MUCH SHALL WE GIVE?

In our zeal for benevolences we must not forget that our first duty is the maintenance of our Church." This plea in a 1917 Sunday bulletin, meant to encourage pew rentals, may sound miserly to current members who would raise mission giving beyond 20 percent. In the 1910s, however, benevolence sometimes surpassed operating expenses, not counting the funds raised by the women's missionary societies.

Pew rentals, supplemented by pledges and special appeals to deep-pocketed members, paid the bills, but pew renters were not spared the collection plate. Each Sunday's offering was designated for a particular mission, and its advocates urged generosity. Mission was so central to Westminster's identity that church officers were offended by the large assessments from Presbytery for its mission endeavors.

How generous have we been?

Local Benevolences from the 1920 Budget		in 2007 dollars
Riverside Chapel	$ 11,250	$115,594
Hope Chapel	8,500	87,338
Anti-Saloon League	475	4,881
Faith Chapel Kindergarten	1,500	15,413
Macalester College	1,000	10,275
Union City Mission	250	2,569

(not including payments to Presbyterian boards, women's mission benevolences, Abbott Hospital, or money disbursed directly by the Session Fund or the Trustees Fund)

Above right: A detail from a stained glass window on the Twelfth Street wall in the sanctuary depicting the Sermon on the Mount.

At right: As a church officer and as Community Outreach Worker in the 1980s-90s, Phyllis Sutton established new partnerships in local mission and kept social justice issues before the congregation.

By 1920 the church used a budget system that centralized all spending except the women's funds. Not knowing where one's dollars would wind up may have dampened the congregation's zeal somewhat. The Depression of the 1930s took a hit on the budget, but still benevolences stayed above 21 percent.

The benevolence portion of the church's outlay fell in the 1950s and hit bottom at 9 percent in 1970. Women's Association funds were added in for the first time to inflate the sorry figure to 13 percent. Was Westminster attracting stingier worshipers? Had our space and personnel needs grown so expensive that there was nothing left for others? In 1957 with benevolences at 15 percent, Dr. Lowe announced that Westminster ranked third in giving among downtown churches in the United States.

Broader social trends must account for some of the drop. Anti-colonial movements ended or altered the foreign missions long popular with church donors. New Deal social supports, organized labor, a postwar industrial boom, the G.I. Bill, and affordable suburban housing narrowed the gap between rich and poor. The poor were still with us, but their image had changed since the days when charity aided working-class immigrant families. The poor most visible to Westminster worshipers slept in the bushes or panhandled in the parking lot: homeless men, many suffering from alcoholism or mental illness. Presbyterian benevolence didn't produce miracles.

Walter (Rocky) Rockenstein, ordained an elder in 1975 and assigned to the Outreach Council, was chagrined to learn that benevolence stood at 12 percent of expenses. The church his father served as pastor in West Virginia had set an "aspirational goal" of one-third and expected at least 20 percent each year. Rockenstein found other elders zealous to raise the figure. Andrew Hobart won Session's agreement to a goal of 20 percent to be achieved in increments, but how to calculate the figure remained in dispute. The 1977 budget merely moved the denomination's assessments from the Administration category to Benevolences, even though not all the money went to mission. For the next five years, Hobart worked toward a formula that set the benevolence goal at 25 percent of pledge income, excluding denominational assessments. The formula has been altered many times since.

Rockenstein saw an opportunity to boost giving when Session received the Trustees' plan for the 1978 Major Fund Drive. He proposed that it include a percentage for benevolence. Session amended the plan to say, "If possible, a proportionate amount of the earnings will be used for mission each year." Even that vague an intention caused some behind-the-scenes scurrying, and the amendment was soon undone.

Debates over benevolence funding often pitted the Board of Deacons, responsible for local mission, against Session, the governing body, and Session against Trustees, the stewards of the church's money. A recession in 1989 threw everyone's best intentions into conflict but also showed that Westminster has the wherewithal for generous mission support. First, the Counseling Center asked the Trustees for $17,000 to cover losses, and the Trustees asked the Mission Committee to bear half that cost.

Then increases in the Social Security tax and health and pension benefits delayed an associate pastor search. The proposed budget reduced benevolence by $23,835 to offset increases elsewhere. Session asked the Trustees to draw that sum from the endowment, but the Trustees could not "in good conscience" comply. In a close vote Session spared the Trustees' consciences, provided they brought the issue to the congregation. A "Close the Benevolence Gap" campaign complete with envelopes was announced at the congregational meeting on January 28, 1990. By February 22 more than $26,000 had been raised.

A pastoral crisis in the late 1990s led Westminster to renew its zeal for mission. A double-tithe of 20 percent of total expenses has been achieved. With the leadership of Gretchen Musicant and Fred Dietrich, mission programs were gathered into a Faith in Action Council that coordinates benevolence spending with hands-on mission and social justice advocacy, and an associate pastor, Douglas Mitchell, was called in 2001 to lead the effort. Each year Mitchell, the Council co-chairs, and the chairs of the Council's five ministry teams meet to divide the benevolence funds. A clergy observer asked for her impression of the process declared, "There are a bunch of Christians in that room."

Rocky Rockenstein got a second chance to link benevolence to capital campaigns. As co-chairs of the campaign that funded the sanctuary restoration and the 2002 addition, he and Carol Mae Olson succeeded in getting an amount equal to 20 percent of building costs dedicated to mission. Through this "Mission Component formula", which also affects the 150th Anniversary Campaign, "the church models for its members the concept of giving generously out of the abundance God provides." ✚

At left: Children from the Carl, Rusler, McLellan, and Van Hulzen families prepare Christmas gifts.

Above: Second-graders Morgan Christianson and Mariel de Vries Jones collect funds to buy honeybees through Heifer Project International in 2005.

A WELCOME LESSON

*"You enter this church
not as a stranger but as a
child of God."*

A statement printed in the Sunday bulletin for many years.

WELCOME TO WESTMINSTER!

Between the revival meetings of the early twentieth century and the team ministry plan of Vision 2000, the word "evangelism" fell out of habitual use at Westminster. Even the Reverend Annika Lister Stroope, called in 2002 to be the Associate Pastor for Evangelism and Fellowship, was at first uneasy with the term's potential to scare away the tentative. But genuine evangelism begins with hospitality, and she treasures her role as "the human welcome mat at Westminster."

Founding members Andrew and Sarah Oliver modeled a generous hospitality. Every Sunday morning they hitched their pair of mules to a rockaway or a sled and made the rounds of frontier Minneapolis, inviting aboard anyone who wished a ride to church. Deacon Oliver also welcomed and ushered newcomers into prime seats. William and Elmira Ankeny invited worshipers to their home for fellowship after the morning service.

Although a beautiful church is itself an invitation to worship, the need to maintain it sometimes made Westminster look inhospitable. The pew rental system of financing adopted in the 1870s made it difficult to seat visitors comfortably. After a discussion in 1901 of "the necessity of making the public feel that Westminster Church welcomes strangers to its services," a large, bold "ALL ARE WELCOME" appeared on the cover of the Sunday bulletin. Of course you first had to come inside to find that out.

As members moved farther away and grew reluctant to make two Sunday trips, the church looked to its evening service as a fruitful time to welcome "the masses of this great city." A 1906 study recommended that this service be "evangelistic in character, with a view to attracting and saving the great floating population around the church." Just who was floating at Twelfth and Nicollet wasn't specified.

The "masses" grew considerably after World War I with migration from rural areas to the city. Wesley Methodist Church surveyed the neighborhood in 1919 and found more than sixty thousand people living within eight blocks' reach, 45 percent with no church home. Westminster adopted new welcoming strategies: outdoor lighting, displays for hotel counters, newspaper ads, doorway greeters, a card to fill in and leave in the collection plate, an organ recital before the evening service, members strategically seated to greet strangers, and a new slogan, "A friendly church . . . Try it!" The evening service could filter the newcomers and turn some into morning pew renters. Assistant Pastor Harry Strock followed up with home and work visits to involve new members in the life of the church.

Young, single working women who moved to town in the 1920s found a welcome at the morning service. A block of pews in the right balcony was reserved for Mrs. Strock's Bible Class and "any young woman who, like themselves, has no family in >>>

Above right: A Westminster picnic in Peavey Plaza in the 1980s.

Dr. Lowe's following was especially constrained by pew rentals, and in 1956 he recommended suspending this "spiritual hindrance" that "cannot be considered either Christian or democratic." The following year membership reached an all-time high of 3,980. Two other changes, temporary and not fully supported initially, have since become mainstays of Westminster's welcome: Assistant Pastor Henry Chace began an optional Inquirers class, and Westminster Service Guild offered an experimental coffee and fellowship hour after worship.

The 1960s-70s brought changes to Westminster's neighborhood that tested its openness and its self-perception. Urban renewal in the Gateway displaced single men from low-cost housing along Washington Avenue and drove them southward, where construction of Interstate 94 had temporarily lowered the value of the remaining rentals. Westminster's new neighbors were seen not as prospective members but as objects of its benevolence. A transient ministry supplied them with meal vouchers or tokens for the Medicine Lake bus, which took them to Jerry Paul's Mission Farm for housing and work. Other churches, too, faced the question, "What of Those Living in the Church's Shadow?" the headline on a 1965 *Tribune* article in a series, "The Downtown Church: How Strong?" While forty thousand people lived downtown, "fewer than 10 percent of the family units at Westminster Presbyterian Church reside within a mile of the church," the article reported. "Most downtown churches consciously approach religion from an intellectual point of view, while the people living there have the lowest median educational level in the city."

The extension of Nicollet Mall and the Greenway to Loring Park promised luxury living within walking distance of the church. The excitement about these new neighbors raised an important identity question: Who is Westminster? Was it, as one local magazine

>>>

Minneapolis and consequently no regular sitting in Westminster." Ida Seymour, the pastor's assistant, led a Girls' Club to offer them fellowship, and they found their place of usefulness in the Westminster Service Guild.

Nothing draws crowds like stellar preaching, and Dr. Burrell in the 1880s and Dr. Lowe from 1941-65 won record attendance. Listeners are not all joiners, however. Early in Lowe's tenure the bulletin carried a quiet notice, "Dr. Lowe will be in his study following the

morning worship. He will be happy to see those who are interested in coming into the church." Later, notices of upcoming new member receptions packed a one-two punch, a challenge followed by a warning. A 1950 bulletin offers, "The conditions of membership in our church are simple but serious. They are the earnest intention to accept Christ as Lord and Master and the endeavor to walk by his teachings to the utmost of our light and strength." The next week the notice reads, "These are days of decision. Men and women must decide where they stand. Neutrality in any matter which affects the well-being of mankind has become a sin."

> *"Jesus went to the city. He had all the reasons in the world not to go to Jerusalem and He did. Churches that are in the city need to reflect that example that Jesus gave of facing the city and all the ugliness and the beauty that can be there. Amen!"*
> Rev. Annika Lister Stroope

gushed, the church to be seen in? How hospitable was the church, really? A tale that Dr. Meisel told on himself one Sunday shows how a church's self-perception shapes its welcome. A woman who sat near the front of the sanctuary every Sunday had come up to him the week before and asked why he urged people to volunteer to serve the F.E.A.S.T. dinner but never invited anyone to eat. Did he think no one in the congregation was poor and hungry? She lived on disability, and her resources stretched thin by the end of the month. She was glad for that Sunday meal. Dr. Meisel gratefully altered his announcement of F.E.A.S.T.

Westminster proclaims itself "a welcoming and caring Christian community" of increasing diversity. Still, how the welcome gets communicated is a practical issue. The Time for Sharing pad introduced in 1975, now the Friendship pad, allows timid newcomers to make their presence known. The china cups with red logos for visitors and green for members have been retired. Coffee servers found few gracious ways to say, No, not that cup! New challenges demand Rev. Stroope's attention: "No minister even twenty years ago could have imagined that any of his or her time would go to talking about, Well, could we have a link underneath the drop down text in the left hand toolbar of the web page homepage?"

Three strategies have proven effective after 150 years. The first is old-fashioned, face-to-face hospitality. When the membership team led by Ray Williams and Molly Parry introduced what they claimed was "the largest new member class of this century," sixty people, in December 1986, their success was due to vigorous personal discipleship. A familiar face at the head of the aisle can turn stranger into friend, as the ushers attest. "I find that sometimes we're the only people in the church who know what's going on," Barbara Mauk says about keeping tabs on the "little community" that sits in her section. "I think having the same people usher as often as possible is a vital, vital ministry in the church."

The second strategy, instruction in Presbyterian faith and polity, leads newcomers to the next phase of evangelism, "accepting and understanding the commitments called for in the Covenant of Membership. One of my responsibilities as a pastor," Stroope explains, "is to say, You have to make a commitment, and it is not going to be easy and it is going to take time." A series of classes designed by the Member Development Committee smoothes that process.

Finally, clarity about the church's purpose signals to visitors that this is a congregation to count on. "Westminster's future needs to be perpetually in dialogue with the city that we live in," Stroope believes, "and to listen to it as well as to speak to it prophetically. The city comes to our doorstep in many different ways. Jesus went to the city. He had all the reasons in the world not to go to Jerusalem and He did. Churches that are in the city need to reflect that example that Jesus gave of facing the city and all the ugliness and the beauty that can be there. Amen!" ✦

Westminster welcomes all believers to its communion table, regardless of church membership or denomination. Individual communion cups were first used in 1905.

From stranger to Clerk of Session
VINCE THOMAS

Tim Hart-Andersen and Vince Thomas remove a 104-year-old time capsule from the church's cornerstone in preparation for the re-dedication of the sanctuary in October 2000. The contents, quite water-damaged, are now in the church archives.

Vincent Thomas moved to Minneapolis in 1986, fresh out of law school at twenty-five, for a job with a downtown firm. "I had no community here at all," he recalls. A "cradle Presbyterian," he hoped to find a church like his home church: beautiful, historic Fort Street Presbyterian in downtown Detroit. He had heard that Westminster was the place. Week after week he rushed in at 10:25 a.m., took a seat in the balcony, then hurried out after the service.

Dr. Meisel's sermons engaged him, and the hymns and choral responses were familiar, but the congregation's size and wealth felt intimidating. And Minneapolis wasn't Detroit. "Minneapolis is a great city," Thomas says. "I love it. But it's a difficult town in which to be a single black man." Although he hadn't grown up in a typically African American worship tradition, he didn't relish feeling isolated at church. He was already the only black lawyer in his firm. Nevertheless, church-shopping expeditions kept bringing him back to Westminster.

One Sunday "this older Euro-American woman, silver hair, very nice" introduced herself as Lee Williams and asked him about himself. She located two families from Detroit sitting a few rows behind him, Cathie and Gerry Fischer and Mervin and Geraldine Winston. The hometown connection felt reassuring, and the Winstons were African American. Sitting with the Fischers and/or the Winstons became his Sunday pattern. "I had people looking out for me, and I found myself looking forward to seeing them."

Still it took him nearly two years to join. "I had to be sure it was a place where I was really going to be a welcomed member of the community," Thomas explains. "Euro-Americans, even church folks, have the same history of their country that I have. Some may look on me with wariness solely because I am African American." Dr. Meisel's sermon on "waiting in high gear" and Cathie Fischer's direct "When are you going to join?" ended his hesitation. He soon volunteered as a youth group adviser.

Thomas had become an elder at Fort Street Church at fifteen, so he went forward for the laying-on of hands when officers were ordained at Westminster. Dr. Meisel "stunned" him by asking if he would finish the term of an elder who had resigned. During his first full term on Session, at thirty-two, his name was put forward to succeed Art Nelson as Clerk. Thomas often thinks of a predecessor who served as Clerk of Session for thirty-four years: "I could serve for as long as Charles Telford Thompson did and still feel like I haven't repaid Westminster. Now it's not just the church that welcomed me. It's the church where I met my wife, where we were married, where our children were baptized."

It is easy to put a happy ending on Vince Thomas's story. He is proud to be Westminster's first African American Clerk of Session, especially for what that means to his parents, raised in the segregated South. His clerkship is a beginning and a challenge: "Even though I love the Westminster community, there are still times when I feel isolated. I have a family around me that I didn't have before. But I'm human, and the reality is that there aren't very many other people like me here, and there are times when I wish that weren't the case." ✚

Children in church

"OF SUCH IS THE KINGDOM OF GOD"
Mark 10:14

"Papa and I went to the evening service and heard Dr. Burrell preach a good sermon to about 1700 people. Many were turned away." Ezra Fitch Pabody, Jr.

Ten-year-old Fitch Pabody filled his 1882 diary with accounts of cocoons tended, his desire for an aquarium, and his muscle-building regimen, but also his family's church attendance, Dr. Sample's sermon texts, and progress on the Seventh Street building. The centrality of church in his life echoed the childhoods of Sam and Josh Williams a generation earlier. Sunday worship gathered everyone in the auditorium, as the sanctuary was called. Only after the ninety-minute service did they divide by age, gender, and marital status into Sabbath school classes. Fitch often came back to church Sunday night and always on Thursday evenings unless he was sick. Then he and his mother would have their "own little prayer meeting" at home.

Children's Day services on the second Sunday in June, designated by General Assembly, featured the children's voices and their knowledge of Sabbath school lessons. Westminster's was moved to the last Sunday in May in 1904 because so many families had already "retired to their lake homes." At the Pabody cottage in Excelsior, "Papa" read a sermon to the family on summer Sundays.

A gradual exodus of children from worship began before Fitch Pabody turned fifty. The April 1919 *Westminster News* announced, "A long-felt need of our church has finally been met with the establishment of a playroom for the children of parents who desire to attend the morning service at Westminster. >>>

A church school class in the 1970s.

123

>>>

Under the efficient supervision of Miss Mildred Hicks and Miss Helen Burchard this play room is open to children of all ages and is equipped with toys and games for the entertainment of all." No explanation is offered for why children, welcome in worship for six decades, should be dismissed and occupied with toys rather than their own little prayer meetings.

Playroom attendance wasn't mandatory and didn't appeal to all families. Our older members recall sitting in church with their parents. Later announcements specify "a nursery for young children." By the mid-1920s concern shifted to young adolescents in worship. A separate Junior Church began meeting at the 11:00 a.m. worship time, with its order of worship printed in the Sunday bulletin, and continued through the 1930s. Church school met at 9:45 a.m..

Research into psychology had begun lining out stages of development that differentiated children's spiritual needs from adults'. Westminster kept up with the trends. Herman Sweet, Director of Religious Education from 1926 to 1938, ran the program according to "scientific methods." Church school, "a socializing process," eased up on memorization of Bible verses to become "a joyful and satisfying experience."

> *"We believe that Church should be associated in the child's mind with a sense of well-being, friendliness, and pleasant activity,"* *Sweet wrote. "Only then will that which is learned become strong in its motivating influence." Children were perhaps less motivated by sermons than previously thought.*

The separation of children and adults widened at Westminster in the 1940s when church school was rescheduled to coincide with worship. Some other downtown churches made the same change. Even Children's Day was relocated to the Great Hall and held before worship. The growth of suburbs after World War II placed middle-class white children in domestic enclaves distant from the public life of the city, and in 1952 Westminster built its own suburb, an education wing with an architectural layout both actually and

Dr. Meisel was known for his fine attention
to detail, even in the children's sermons.
One Sunday he brought a birthday cake with
trick candles to illustrate a lesson about
Jesus as the Light of the World. The kids,
as instructed, blew and blew and blew.
Dr. Meisel had overlooked one detail, the
coconut in the frosting, which wound up all
over his ministerial robe.

symbolically remote from the sanctuary. Yet the children were not deprived.
They had eager, well-trained teachers. A full complement of children's choirs
nurtured a love of sacred music, which they could occasionally bring to the
sanctuary. Lloyd Peitzman brought a new energy to Christian Education and
youth fellowship in 1962, along with the latest audio and video technology.

By the late 1970s change was astir. The early baby boomers were getting
married and starting families more child-centered than the previous
generation's. These parents wanted opportunities for family worship. Joey
Rockenstein remembers, "Westminster was not a comfortable or at least not
an easy place to have young children. From the atmosphere and the attitude
of the ushers we did not feel that children were welcome in the worship
service, certainly not children who made any noise." The Christian Education
program wanted children to experience sanctuary worship on occasion as
a learning tool. One solution was to invite them into church periodically,
let their choirs sing, offer them a children's sermon, and then dismiss them
to church school. Some congregants drawn to Westminster precisely by
the adult decorum of its worship were, however, displeased. An article in
the *Westminster News* of February 8, 1982, addressed this group with an
analogy: "Bringing children into worship is something like letting them eat at
table even though their table manners are less than great."

A motion to separate the worship and church school hours failed in
Session in 1982, but a five-year effort to create a ministry for children and
families succeeded in 1985. Under the dramatic, creative leadership of the
Reverend David Strandin, children's programming blossomed. "David didn't
do anything small," Karen Gasche, who chaired the Christian Education
Committee, recalls. "He did everything large, larger than life."

Sharon Engel had been hired to revitalize the children's choirs, and their
practice night, Wednesday, was turned into family night at church with
supper and a wide choice of activities. As participation grew so did the
desire to integrate children into the heart of the church. >>>

Rev. David Strandin served from 1985-89 as
the first ordained pastor for children and
families. A mix of fatherly compassion and
boyish glee, he was as comfortable in a clown
suit as in a clerical robe. Less than four years
after accepting a call to Indiana, he passed
away from cancer on January 26, 1993. His
wife, Carol, and daughters, Cassandra and
Blythe, returned for a memorial service, where
many members of the congregation rose to
offer testimony and tell stories.

From left to right: In 1971 General Assembly passed an overture allowing children "of Christian homes" to take communion. Westminster welcomed the children as long as their parents were present and the children had been taught about the sacrament. Here Lloyd Peitzman, Director of Christian Education at that time, instructs a group of confirmands.

Gina Gustavson, who grew up at Westminster and directed the nursery from 1984-96, cuddles two of her charges, whom she remembers as Justin and George.

Children, Honor Your Library

During the 1980s renovation a decision was made not to include children's books in the new Lowe Library. The beautiful Prairie School room that the architects Purcell and Elmslie designed in 1910 for the primary Sunday school was to be adults-only. Nor were there plans for a children's library. Three members of the Library Committee, Joey Rockenstein, Maxine Sinclair, and Midge Brown, became "verbal and persistent and stubborn" about a central space for children's books. To enlist congregational support Rockenstein found a book cart, loaded it with children's books to lend, and wheeled it into the coffee hour Sunday after Sunday. "It was a bit pushy, I suppose," she admits, but it worked. "We did manage to get the ideal spot for it." A room intended for kitchen storage was made available. Their final achievement was the door between the libraries that allows parents and kids to check on each other.

>>>

A clash of cultures within the congregation erupted each Easter from 1986 through 1988 over the presence of the children's choirs in the sanctuary. Some members objected to letting children "perform" in a setting designed for worship, especially if their singing fell short of Westminster's standard of excellence. Rev. Strandin explained that singing in the big church on festival days was indeed worship from the child's point of view.

It took a long-range plan to bring children back to worship. A broad-based Task Force on the Sunday Schedule appointed in 1990 examined the issues involved. The difficulty of recruiting church school teachers willing to sacrifice worship helped make the case for change, as did the possibility of a full adult education program. David Strandin had accepted a pastorate in Indiana, so the Reverend Erwin Barron, called in 1990 as Associate Minister for Children and Families and Adult Education, took on the role of children's advocate. Rev. Barron says that the tradition-minded adults were easier to persuade than the "peripheral parents," the ones who showed up now and then to drop their kids off in church school so they could go to church unencumbered.

The schedule inaugurated in September 1991 included a 9:00 a.m. service in the sanctuary with lay leadership, associate pastors preaching, and "child-friendly" worship; a 9:45 education hour for all ages; and an 11:00 formal service with children in church at the start. The plan proved short-lived. The Reverend David Philpott, who served as interim pastor after Dr. Meisel's retirement in 1992, feared the church would divide into two incompatible

Olivia and Ava Bruhn greet their senior pastor, Tim Hart-Andersen.

congregations. Considerable discussion and a member survey led to a brief service at 8:30, a 9:15 education hour, and 10:30 worship.

Turning Westminster back into a true family church required a major evaluation of the church's long-term prospects. David Koehler, who chaired the committee that called the Reverend Timothy Hart-Andersen as pastor, recalls that as they drew up the job description and the church profile, they had to decide whether to affirm Westminster's identity as an "adult church, a downtown Protestant cathedral" or seek a pastor who would "draw young families to worship and fill up the Sunday school with young children." They chose to list an emphasis on working with children and families as one of three primary ideals.

Perhaps the best case for integrating children into the life of the church comes from Barbara Knight Coffin, who sat in the front pew in the 1920s-30s: "I think a lot of the children at the time that I grew up had a real sense of ownership of the church. We felt it was our church and we were proud that we were part of it. Also I felt like the older people in the church were fond of me. Adults would make a special effort to know me and to notice little important things I had done. In a similar way I was fond of them. They were my world in those days: Dr. Bushnell, sweet old Dr. Bushnell who was my childhood minister, and Mr. and Mrs. Herman Sweet, Jennie Congdon, Rewey Belle Inglis, and Mrs. Baker, my nursery teacher. Even the ones I wasn't fond of were part of my world. I think it's important for adults in the church to remember how important they are to kids." ✧

Who is that guy?

The choir had sung the final verse of the processional hymn on a Sunday morning in the 1980s and taken their seats. One of the altos let out a *sotto voce* sigh. "Mister Rogers," she swooned. Her pew mates went into where? where? mode and scanned the congregation without visibly moving their heads. There indeed sat the beloved Fred Rogers of children's television, an ordained Presbyterian minister. The news was ventriloquized and mimed to the mothers throughout the choir. The congregation, except for those seated near him, was none the wiser. After church he shook hands with Dr. Meisel and went his way, without changing his shoes. His core fans off in the nursery and Sunday school never saw him.

BAPTISM THROUGH THE YEARS

Among Barbara Knight Coffin's memories is a fond image of baptism in the 1920s: "George Dayton, Grandpa Dayton, a very dignified, nice-looking man with short, straight white hair and white beard, led in the couples with their babies, carrying a bowl of water. The minister would come down and stand right in front of where we sat. The minister would take each baby in his arms and baptize them using the water from the bowl that Grandpa Dayton carried. Then the babies were transferred back into their parents' arms and carried out."

Nothing wreaks havoc on a lovely sacramental ritual like a baby boom. At the Children's Day service June 10, 1951, Dr. Lowe baptized twenty-three babies, including current deacon Doris Wong. Baptisms were soon relegated to the chapel, to a special service for the families, and they stayed there until Dr. Bates's first baptism in 1965. Eighteen babies turned up that day, and parents were subsequently given a choice of chapel or sanctuary baptism. By 1968 they were back in the sanctuary, in view of the congregation that promises to nurture the children in their faith.

Top to bottom:
Rev. John Bates with a baptismal family.

Confirmands in the 1970s (Nancy Etzwiler, *left*) study the relief on the baptismal font.

Rev. Erwin Barron with Marc and Sonja Zapchenk and daughter Hannah, baptized in 1993.

In the adult atmosphere of worship in the 1980s baptisms were quick and efficient. The babies were whisked in one door, blessed with one hand, and whisked out the other door. When Rev. Erwin Barron came on staff as Associate Pastor for Children and Families in 1990, he insisted that baptism be done by the book, *The Book of Order.* The parents must be Westminster members ready to raise their children in the church, and the congregation must be impressed with the seriousness of its commitment. Holding the babies and introducing them to their spiritual guardians became a vital piece of the ritual.

Today's team ministry approach to baptism allows for at least as many babies as clergy. As the ministers wander up the aisles to allow the congregation a good look, some child is storing up a favorite image to describe eighty years hence. ✛

When Lorraine Purdy came to Westminster in 1948, Rupert Sircom admitted her to the choir and paid her a small sum that she gave back to the church, as many other singers did. Five years later Bryce and Lola Barnes joined the choir without pay. A reduction in the oft-disputed music budget, perhaps, turned a professional ensemble into a membership-based choir. Sircom's rehearsals were "all business," Bryce Barnes remembers, but that isn't the whole truth. There was joking in the locker rooms, and some of the men would climb out the window to smoke on the slate roof. Singing with Sircom was an experience to treasure. "We got a babysitter every Wednesday night," Lola Barnes recalls. "That was our night out, going to choir practice." Sircom excelled as choirmaster and as organist, a rare combination no longer expected. "Rupert had it all," Purdy says.

Edward Berryman admitted singers with good voices even if they couldn't sight-read, so rehearsals required more drills. The choir nearly doubled in size, and the overflow group in the balcony stood on the stairs to keep the sound even. "The stairs curve somewhat," Sandra Berthene points out, "so the treads are narrower toward the curve, and there is no handrail. I really don't like those steps." "What I liked about Ed," Bryce says, "was if one of the parts, the baritones, were having trouble with something, he would play that part on the organ, even though it wasn't written in there, to bail us out. I can't imagine anyone who had as much music memorized as that guy did." Berryman could also transpose music freely into any key.

They deem Peter Hendrickson more choir director than organist and appreciate his tenure for the repertoire he brought and the challenge of singing in German. Berthene tells of singing Brahms's *Ein Deutsches Requiem* to a near capacity house at Orchestra Hall. Purdy was not happy when Hendrickson omitted "This Glad Easter Day," sung every Easter since 1932, like its Christmas counterpart, "What a Wonder." "There are some things that are traditional and should be left alone, but these young people don't see it that way."

By all testimony, Stephen Sheftz was an outstanding choir director, with an ear so fine that he could hear, as Berthene describes it, "if there was a variation in the way a section was pronouncing a particular syllable, if there was somebody indulging in what he called 'scoopando,' scooping up on the tone, or somebody was a quarter tone flat." They enjoyed his selection of "almost avant garde" music that challenged the choir to become good sight-readers.

Purdy missed Westminster in the years she lived elsewhere, and she was sorry to have to leave the choir after a stroke, but she is happy to have had thirty-nine years of top-notch singing experience. The Barneses retired in 2003 after fifty years and are pleased to have sung with the current team, Melanie Ohnstad, Minister of Music and the Arts, at the organ, and Jere Lantz directing the choir. Bryce calls Lantz "the easiest director to follow that I've ever seen. If you watch him, you know exactly what to do." Berthene, who doubles as choir librarian, credits her training in the choir, supplemented by voice lessons with Marian Hoffman, the soprano soloist now retired, for keeping her vocal cords in fine enough shape to sing as she grows older. ✤

AN ACCESSIBLE CHURCH

Founder Louis Williams was nearly blind and his brother Joseph "frail." Andrew Oliver was so lame in his fifties that a parishioner described his ushering as "a painful process to all concerned." Yet Westminster built churches for the robust, with grand entry stairways, vast spaces, raised pulpits and choir lofts, and second story classrooms. Ministry to "shut-ins" who couldn't get into the church occupied assistant pastors and volunteers.

Since the mid-twentieth century, medical advances have turned many terminal, waste-away diseases into chronic disabling conditions that allow a purposeful life. The Civil Rights movement established the idea that excluding anyone from civic life because of a natural attribute is unjust. Westminster's youth felt that injustice keenly in the 1970s when Associate Pastor Ellen Babinsky set them up for a "handicapped lock-in." Negotiating the church and its neighborhood blindfolded or in wheelchairs aroused their sense of fairness and sent them to the Trustees to ask why the church couldn't at least have an elevator. The Centennial campaign fund in 1957 had included plans for one, but it took nearly thirty years to appear. When remodeling moved the main office to the second floor and added a ramped entrance to the neighboring bank's underground parking, an elevator looked essential even to the fit. Dedication day was May 9, 1985.

Drama can identify a problem, but solving it takes persistent advocacy. At Westminster persistence is embodied in Lois Hietala, who joined the Presbytery Disabilities Concerns Committee in the 1980s after a neurological illness ended her church school teaching: She couldn't get to the classrooms. Among the improvements that Hietala's "push, push, praise" approach has accomplished are level spaces for wheelchairs in the sanctuary, a note in the bulletin that reads, "Please stand, if you are able," the railing along the pulpit stairs, non-slip tile, a lowered drinking fountain, the wheelchair-high section of the reception desk, and increased handicap parking.

Hietala has helped the church architects and property managers think beyond the legal building code to the congregation's particular needs. One day she arranged a demonstration and asked John Greenwald, who uses an electric wheelchair, to come to church in his usual fashion—wheeling up the ramp, ringing the doorbell, and waiting for someone to help him in. Sam Cooke and Al Cooper stood by and contemplated what it would take for Greenwald to get inside on his own. The result is the automatic door at the chapel entrance installed in 1996, which illustrates an added challenge for a historic church like Westminster. "You couldn't put just any old door in there," Hietala explains. "You had this gorgeous arch, and so it had to conform to that. It cost the church a small fortune, I'm sure." (A memorial fund from the family of Harold and Ruth Finch paid the bill.) She credits the Reverend Gordon Stewart and Trustee Jim Tillitt with respecting her vision of a fully accessible church in the design of the new education wing opened in 2002.

The vision is not yet realized. The pulpit is still a climb, and the congregation could think of disability in broader terms than limited mobility. Presbytery's new Disabilities Concerns Task Force is studying accessibility for the mentally ill. "It's one thing to get in the door," Hietala says, "but it's another thing to participate." Is Westminster's high standard of decorum a barrier for the developmentally disabled or for those whose mental illnesses affect their social behavior? ✛

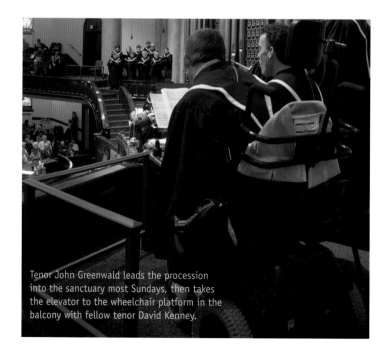

Tenor John Greenwald leads the procession into the sanctuary most Sundays, then takes the elevator to the wheelchair platform in the balcony with fellow tenor David Kenney.

After long and painful reflection, a talented young woman with a vocational pull toward the church decided to withdraw from seminary and end her candidacy for ministry. Suzanne Rekow's carefully worded letter was read at the September 1996 Session meeting: "I can no longer continue to give my time, talents, money and energy to a church that considers me and so many others unworthy of ordination." As a lesbian in a committed relationship, she knew there was little hope for ordination in the Presbyterian Church.

Her decision evoked an outpouring of sympathy from elders. That same evening Session decided in a nearly unanimous vote to oppose an amendment to the Presbyterian *Book of Order* known as Amendment B, which would require all ordained persons to maintain "fidelity in marriage and chastity in singleness." Approved by General Assembly just months before and undergoing ratification by presbyteries, Amendment B in effect barred from ordained office all sexually active gay men and lesbians, even those within long-term, monogamous relationships.

The elders' action did not prevent the Amendment's ratification and addition to The *Book of Order* as G-6.0106b, and it came too late to alter Rekow's decision. It did, however, signal the start of a more activist stance at Westminster on issues affecting gay, lesbian, bisexual, and transgendered people and an increasing willingness to place principles over propriety.

Since the 1970s, when the gay pride movement drew attention to the discrimination gay people faced in all areas of life, nearly every mainstream Protestant tradition has divided over such issues as homosexual marriage and ordination. Among Presbyterians the debates have been fierce and still threaten to split the denomination, despite a historic commitment to respectful dialogue. Westminster's congregation is frequently reminded of the "Historic Principles" set forth at the founding of the American denomination in 1788: "That God alone is Lord of the conscience . . . there are truths and forms with respect to which people of deep faith may differ." (G-1.0300)

The debate has stirred deep-seated conflicts simmering since the early twentieth century over the nature of truth and Biblical authority: "[It] illustrates that the denomination has never truly recovered from the effects of the Fundamentalist-Modernist controversy . . . the same tension has come back to haunt us in a new form," Paul Capetz, a professor at United Theological Seminary, observes. Homosexuality has replaced evolution as the divisive subject.

The PCUSA first took a stand on gay and lesbian ordination in 1978, when General Assembly issued a "definitive guidance" declaring that "unrepentant, practicing" homosexual persons should not be ordained. Some presbyteries questioned the meaning of definitive guidance and rejected it as non-binding. Westminster's approach was cautious. The Church and Society Committee sponsored a series of conversations, but took no public stand. Session appointed a task force to study the question but never >>>

The "Shower of Stoles" project was displayed at Westminster during the 2002 conference of the Covenant Network. The liturgical stoles are created by gay men and lesbians denied their ministerial roles by the adoption of Amendment B to the Constitution of the PCUSA.

endorsed its findings. The issue simmered through the 1980s and into the 1990s, when Rev. Erwin Barron joined the staff and came out as a gay man selectively to colleagues and parishioners.

Lesbians and gay men have long made a home at Westminster, but it hasn't always been comfortable. "Because so many gay people grew up feeling that religion had rejected them, they rejected religion," admits Rodney Allen Schwartz, who avoided church during his twenties. He first attended a service at Westminster by chance and was "blown away" by the pipe organ, excellent choir, and intelligent preaching. "I think the gay people who are attracted to Westminster come here because of what Westminster does in its mainstream mission." He also found that he could be himself: "I didn't ever feel that I had to come out, but I felt that I was out, and I didn't need to be either embarrassed or ashamed or make excuses for it. This is who I am."

Others recount less accepting attitudes. After a member of Barbara Mauk's family came out as a gay man, he eventually left the church for Plymouth Congregational: "As long as he didn't do anything too flamboyant, or wear the wrong clothes, or whatever, he was welcome. As long as he was benign, he was welcome," Mauk claims. Westminster's decorum could be cloying.

Under the leadership of Rev. Gordon Stewart, who had chaired the PCUSA's Committee on Human Sexuality, efforts were again made to foster study and dialogue on issues of human sexuality, to mixed results. One participant remembers these sessions as unproductive and "peculiar," without a clear rationale. A lesbian recalls her anger at being "the subject of a study, as if I were a virus." Fear of scandal sometimes led to placing a higher priority on financial pledges than on public support for changing ordination standards. The deaths from AIDS of three prominent men in the congregation in 1994 evoked more reflection than any study session. Congregants mourned the loss of their friends Deacon Rick Williams, baritone soloist Jack Jaeger, and Elder Lee Maxfield.

The events of September 1997 caused Westminster to take a closer look at its stance on Amendment B. The resignation of two pastors for sexual misconduct produced awkward conversations about sexual fidelity among ordained ministers. With courageous preaching from the Reverend G. Daniel Little, pastor-in-residence for the interim, Westminster remained firm in its commitment to be a welcoming church. The Pastor Nominating Committee made the search for a national leader on the issue a priority.

Rev. Tim Hart-Andersen's arrival in 1999 deepened the congregation's commitment to be agents of change and a place of reconciliation. The founder of the Covenant Network of Presbyterians, an organization working to eliminate Amendment B from *The Book of Order,* Hart-Andersen believes passionately in the inclusion of gay men and lesbians within the full life of the church: "Nothing Jesus says or does leads me to conclude that God would not call faithful gay and lesbian Presbyterians to ordained office."

In 2004 Session adopted an "interpretive approach" to Amendment B, effectively ending the ban on ordaining gay men and lesbians to the offices of elder and deacon. Westminster's supportive posture is also conveyed through its advertisements in the local gay and lesbian press and participation in the annual Gay Pride Festival. All these changes have made Barbara Mauk hopeful: "I like to think that Westminster is a place of possibilities and communities." Suzanne Rekow, now serving out her vocation as an elementary school teacher, has once again returned to Westminster. ✛

At left: The planning committee for the 2002 conference of the Covenant Network, which was held at Westminster. *Clockwise from top*: Manley Olson, Conference Coordinator Stephanie Meredith, Phil Asgian, Fred Dietrich.

TEST OF RESILIENCE

"A moment of suffering or of brokenness can kill you, or it can be a redemptive moment. It was the latter in this case."

The Reverend G. Daniel Little, pastor-in-residence from 1997-98, reflecting in 2006 on Westminster's experience of crisis.

Pews stacked together for refinishing during the restoration of the sanctuary.

TWO PASTORS RESIGN SUDDENLY

**The Reverend
Gordon Campbell Stewart**

Gordon Stewart began his ministry at Westminster in February 1994, drawn by its commitment to be "a telling presence in the city." He came from a ten-year pastorate at Knox Presbyterian Church in Cincinnati and, before that, years of ecumenical campus ministry. During his three and a half years at Westminster, he preached with eloquence and intelligence about inclusivity and social justice, reoriented Session to allow officers more opportunities for leadership, and began "listening sessions" on topics like sexual orientation. His vision led to a precedent-setting twelve-million-dollar capital campaign to rejuvenate Westminster's aging structure.

At right: Comprehensive church renovation continued in the midst of the upheaval caused by the pastors' resignations. Scaffolding permitted workers to reach the sanctuary ceiling during the 1998 renovation. They discovered that some ceiling plaster had pulled away from its supports and could easily have fallen on worshipers below.

The balcony offered a clear view of the unfolding drama that Sunday, September 28, 1997. The 10:30 a.m. service began like any other. Congregants filed to their seats, glanced over their bulletins, and considered staying for the special information session on the Centennial building plans. The first hint that something was amiss came in the opening processional. Instead of the Reverend Gordon Campbell Stewart, a visiting preacher mounted the podium to strains of "Crown Him with Many Crowns." The announcements offered no explanation. The visitor's sermon topic was the second hint.

Ray Larson, interim Executive Presbyter of the Twin Cities Presbytery, reflected on Genesis 32:22-31 in "A New Identity through the Struggle." Associate Pastor Kathy Michael delivered an impassioned pastoral prayer. Then congregants were asked to stay for an important announcement. As silence fell after the postlude, Rev. Stewart appeared wearing street clothes to read a statement of apology and offer his resignation. Associate Pastor Kay Slaikeu followed. The congregation learned that the two were involved in a personal relationship. >>>

"One of the great benefits to come out of that trauma," Rev. Michael believes, *"was that the laity stepped up and found their voice. I found my voice."*

Near left: Definitely a hard hat area, as the sign warns.

Far left: New pipes for the organ.

At right top: All the church pews were removed to refinish the wood floors in the sanctuary.

At right bottom: Rev. Dan Little, who served Westminster as Pastor-in-Residence from 1997-99, with his wife, Joan.

>>>

From the "outer ring" up in the balcony the scene was startling. In the "inner ring," as Clerk of Session Vince Thomas termed the staff and officers, everything had turned surreal. Staff members had learned of the relationship just days before and were managing feelings of betrayal and anger. Session had met on Saturday to decide a course of action. Thomas and Director of Administration Sam Cooke scrambled to deal with the press coverage. Both were interviewed for WCCO's Monday evening news and cooperated with other press outlets. Local newspapers featured prominent stories the following day, and on October 1 *USA Today* ran a piece in its news roundup.

In her October 2 column for the *Saint Paul Pioneer Press*, Katherine Lanpher remarked on the forthright approach: "Tradition holds that you quietly leave town and let the gossip form little vapor trails in your wake. You don't address the problem head on. . . . going public was a bold break with the protocol of organized religion." In the coming months church leaders continued to be open about the situation, providing regular updates to members on the search for an interim pastor and the Presbytery's disciplinary actions. Clergy planned a service of healing to acknowledge congregants' grief. The Reverend Margaret Thomas, Executive of the Synod of Lakes and Prairies, who preached the Sunday following, fielded dozens of calls from troubled church members. "They're a strong congregation," she told the *Pioneer Press.* "They'll be there for each other."

"One of the great benefits to come out of that trauma," Rev. Michael believes, "was that the laity stepped up and found their voice. I found my voice." Michael and Associate Pastor Byron Thompson, the two remaining clergy, were relatively new. Thompson came as an intern in 1993 and moved into a full-time position in 1996, the same year Michael joined the staff. Westminster was the first ordained pastorate for both. Associate Pastor   >>>

A message of hope and words of reassurance

As Clerk of Session, Vince Thomas was the public face of the church after the sudden resignations of Stewart and Slaikeu in 1997. The first person set to speak to the congregation after their letters were read, he recalled a favorite professor who advised his students to give the jury just two or three simple things to ponder. Thomas resolved to "inform, reassure, and give hope." Hope resided in Westminster's enduring place as "a telling presence in the city," so he invoked that image at the end of this "most difficult speech."

Erwin Barron had recently left. Only Sam Cooke, Director of Administration, and Phyllis Sutton, Director for Outreach, had any length of experience at the church, and Sutton was battling cancer. Unwavering leadership from dozens within the church carried them through. Sunday school classes met, adult education forums continued, and plans for the annual stewardship campaign stayed on track.

In mid-October the Reverend G. Daniel Little arrived to serve as Pastor-in-Residence. Retired from a pastorate in Ithaca, New York, he was nationally respected and had held top posts in the Presbyterian Church. "He was a ballast for us," Michael says. "Dan was probably the best set-up man that we could have had because he dealt directly with conflict," Thompson reflects. "No matter who it was, if Dan called them and they said they had something to talk about, Dan had his notebook and he wrote down everything they said. Everybody knew that they were being heard." Little assured the staff that the outcome would be positive. "Sam, don't worry," Little told Cooke. "This institution is sick, but it isn't cancer, it isn't diabetes. They've got a little cold here, but they're so healthy, this place is going to get through this just fine."

As members look back on that Sunday in September 1997, they may recall singing "The Church's One Foundation." Organist Melanie Ohnstad remembers it keenly: "I didn't want the hymn to end because I knew what was to follow." But what ensued could not extinguish the hymn's timeless message of hope. ✚

Above left: Where a small parking lot and education wing added in the 1950s once stood, bulldozers prepare ground for the new Marquette Avenue addition. Sam Cooke, the church's Director of Administration, took a photograph from the same spot each week to create a slide show of the building on the rise.

Above: During the renovation of the sanctuary, worship services moved to the Great Hall, with the choir singing from risers on stage.

The Church's one Foundation is
Jesus Christ her Lord
She is His new creation
By water and the Word:
From heav'n he came and sought her
To be His holy bride;
With His own blood He bought her,
And for her life He died.

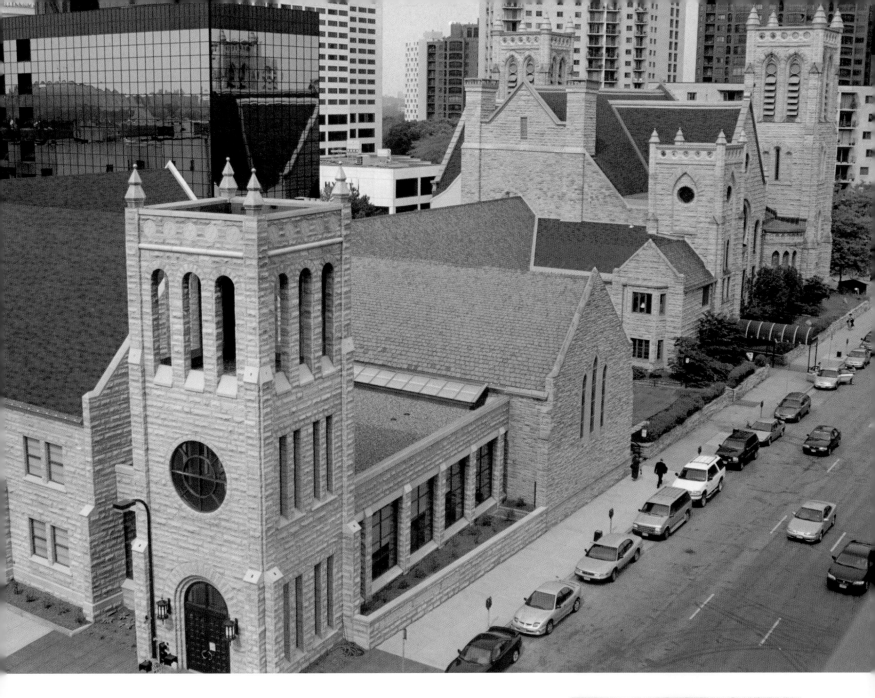

Above: Westminster after the renovation. This photo shows the Twelfth and Marquette entrance to the new program and education wing.

At right: Senior high youth Kirsten Northenscold, Samantha Markey, John Fidler, and Russell Lyons join Rev. Byron Thompson to help lay the cornerstone at the dedication of the Marquette Avenue wing in 2002. Rev. Thompson has since moved on to Westminster's pastoral care ministry, but as the minister with children and families he fine-tuned confirmation to bring youth directly into the active life of the church, and he promoted mission trips across the country for the senior high and into rural Minnesota for the junior high.

139

Once formal affairs, with tables lined up in rigid, schoolhouse fashion, today's Session meetings invite open participation. *Clockwise from window:* Paul Hyde, Rev. Kathy Michael, Jane Norstrom, David Braden, Eric Adams, Susan McKinley, Sandra Berthene, Clerk of Session Vince Thomas (partly hidden), Rev. Tim Hart-Andersen, Rocky Rockenstein.

"W e are not faltering, we are not stopping our capital campaign," Ford Bell told the congregation following Stewart's and Slaikeu's resignations. As chair of the Centennial Committee, he had just helped launch a capital campaign with the unprecedented goal of twelve million dollars to shore up the sagging building and replenish the endowment. All those who had made early commitments stood by their gifts, he reported, and others had pledged new ones. "There was a birth in that moment," Rev. Kathy Michael reflects. "The power of the laity in this congregation" was revealed. At its conclusion, the campaign surpassed its goal by more than two million dollars. A renovated sanctuary and the magnificent Heller Commons and education wing became the physical representation of the laity's vision and persistence.

In many ways Westminster was returning to its roots. Lay leadership built this church. Early parishioners sometimes went months without a pastor. For worship they sang their favorite hymns and read printed sermons. Ministers helped launch key organizations like the Woman's Foreign Missionary Society or the Young People's Society for Christian Endeavor, but laity provided the energy and vision that made them flourish. By the early twentieth century, however, a growing perception of ministers as professionals dampened enthusiasm for lay leadership. In the 1910s Dr. Bushnell lamented a decrease in the number of members willing to lead the Thursday prayer service.

Lay involvement, however, remained strong. Sunday school teachers, hospitality volunteers, and church officers willingly offered their time and talents to help the church run smoothly. But a deferential posture had settled in by the 1940s and remained for several decades, until stirrings of activism in the 1970s-80s focused fresh attention on leadership. >>>

A Call to Discipleship

Since spring 2004 all new deacons, elders and trustees complete a rigorous five-month program that includes study of the Bible, Reformed theology, and church polity; self-reflection and spiritual discernment; and an "apprenticeship" requiring visits to each board. Coordinated by Rev. Kathy Michael and titled "A Call to Discipleship," the program has received overwhelmingly positive responses. Participants have even asked for "more homework." One of the most valuable results has been strengthened relationships among the church's lay leaders.

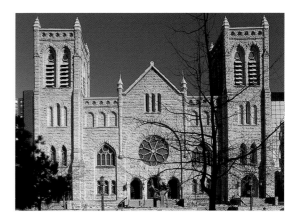

The Nicollet Mall entrance to the sanctuary in the 1990s.

Educational programs were the first area to be renewed. A Lay Academy for adults began in 1975, and lay members working with the Church and Society Committee arranged after-church Open Forums week after week. Today's Social Justice Forum and rich line-up of classes in Education for Faith and Life build on these efforts. Lay advocates brought new initiatives such as refugee sponsorship, socially responsible investing, and hunger programs to the church boards.

Staff positions were also revamped. As a result of a Task Force on Program Staff Organization led by Elder Fred Dietrich in 1991, job descriptions for associate pastors began to emphasize team ministry and lay cooperation. Today, Rev. Michael's area of responsibility is adult education and leadership development, and she encourages members to move from involvement to leadership.

The historic role of Session as a deliberative body received new emphasis during the ministry of Rev. Gordon Stewart, who encouraged active discussion at Session meetings and began listening sessions on controversial topics. After Stewart's departure, Rev. Dan Little made sure that all views were heard before decisions were made. Rev. Tim Hart-Andersen's leadership style reflects a similar commitment: "Everybody needs to speak what they are thinking and contribute to decision-making." In February 2003 the Task Force on Session Size and Function stressed elders' spiritual roles:

"It is the duty of elders, individually and jointly, to strengthen and nurture the faith and life of the congregation committed to their charge," *The Book of Order* reads in G-6.0304.

Rocky Rockenstein marvels at these transitions:

> *"If you look at the number of people here on Sunday morning, it is probably somewhat fewer than when Don [Meisel] was there. But if you take the number of people who are active in the church, that is who aren't just in the pews on Sunday morning, I think the church is a lot better today than it was when I joined it forty years ago. There are more people doing more things both for the congregation and in outreach. That is the result of intentional choices by the leadership to involve more people directly in the activities of the church."* ✦

At left: Session took decisive steps in 2004-05 to ensure that the selection of new officers would be inclusive. The task force responsible for this report undertook a full year of prayerful study and discussion in their efforts to address a divisive issue.

Above: The teaching elders are out of control; time to bring in the ruling elders! *Left to right:* Doug Mitchell, Tim Hart-Andersen, Annika Lister Stroope *(she's really there!)*, Byron Thompson, and Kathy Michael.

AN ACTIVE FAITH

"What does the Lord require of you
but to do justice,
and to love kindness,
and to walk humbly with your God?"

Micah 6:8

The congregation of Familia de Fé, the Twin
Cities Area Presbytery's Hispanic New Church
Development, brings the communion elements
forward for Westminster's World Communion
Sunday in 2006.

COME FOR THE ART, STAY FOR THE GRACE

Top: Peter Lupori, *The Seven Days of Creation,* ceramic, 1981, hangs on a wall just outside the sanctuary opposite the Great Hall. Here are three of the seven tiles.

Bottom: Paul T. Granlund, *The Birth of Freedom,* bronze, 1976, stands in front of the church on Nicollet Mall.

Westminster Church is a work of art with its stained glass windows and elegant woodwork. It also houses a collection of art and historical artifacts. Much of the art accumulated over the years has been of the drive-by-and-drop-off variety: The downsizing of homes has yielded a quantity of antique furniture, for example. The church's acquisition of art turned deliberate in 1975 when the Nicollet Mall was extended past the front entrance. The widened sidewalk called for a sculpture. Elizabeth Heller, Esther Peterson, and other art aficionadas in the congregation invited sculptor Paul T. Granlund to present his work to an audience of possible donors. Thomas and Ella Crosby offered to underwrite a commission based on Galatians 5:1. The public response to *The Birth of Freedom,* discounting objections to its nudity, has proven that art, like music, touches the spirit and draws people to an encounter with the Word.

The opening of the Heller Commons and its gallery space in 2002 has allowed for rotating art exhibitions as well as acquisitions. The facility is aptly named for Elizabeth Heller, now associate pastor emerita. Sunday bulletins from the 1950s-60s announce that Mrs. Heller, not yet Elder or Reverend, is conducting the youth of Westminster Fellowship on a tour of the Minneapolis Institute of Art or discussing with them what modern art has to offer Christianity. Her deep interest in religious art dates to her student days at McCormick Seminary and the influence of Hulda Niebuhr, sister of theologians Reinhold and Richard, and her collection of art prints. "Whenever you were doing field work in a local church," Rev. Heller recalls, "you could go over to her home and pick out what you might use in your Sunday school class."

Historical exhibitions during the Sesquicentennial year have featured artifacts, many from the church's archives, representing cultural changes through the decades of Westminster's life. A new climate-controlled archival space will house the church's textiles, ceramic artifacts, old communion silver, paper documents, and other valuables that have been stored in closets, the attic, and the crawl space under the sanctuary.

The mission that drives the Westminster Gallery and guides its acquisition of art emphasizes cultural diversity and Christianity's global reach. Seeing how people of various ethnicities envision Jesus and interpret stories from the Bible enlarges our understanding of Christian faith. The gallery also seeks art that interests children.

Asked why a church should have an art gallery, Schwartz encourages skeptics to think about pre-literate people, as many Christians have been, and how they have relied on symbols and icons to express their faith. "Art speaks to our soul. It tells us stories. It allows us to meditate, or to consider a subject matter in a very personal way." It also gets people's attention. "Any church is one generation away from closing," he cautions, and Westminster is well located to let art play a role in evangelism. "Come for the art and stay for the grace," Schwartz invites. ✛

Rev. Heller's own collection began with work from art students and emerging artists. As a commissioned church worker in campus ministry at the University of Minnesota, she introduced students to the Japanese printmaker Sadao Watanabe at a time when his prints cost twenty dollars or less. "They were rolled up in a tube and sent through regular mail," she laughs. Today the Westminster Gallery's "art cart" makes frequent trips between Rev. Heller's apartment on LaSalle Avenue and Heller Commons.

Rev. Heller invited Rodney Allen Schwartz to convene a fine art committee and brainstorm uses of the gallery space. He is now on staff part-time as director of the Westminster Gallery. The gallery has showcased art made by Westminster members and disabled artists from the Interact Center and introduced the Chinese Christian artist He Qi and the paintings of Hmong Minnesotan Cy Thao to the congregation. Exhibitions also illustrate seasons of the church year.

He Qi, *Losing Paradise*, gouache on rice paper, 2005. During the Cultural Revolution in China, He Qi painted portraits of Chairman Mao Tse-tung during the day and the Madonna secretly at night. His later art history education in China and Germany led him to a doctorate and a professorship at the Nanjing Union Theological Seminary. He combines traditional Chinese folk customs, materials, and techniques with Western styles of art to produce compelling and brilliantly colored compositions. Storytelling and evangelism come together in a Christian message of peace and joy. He Qi was introduced to Westminster through his friendship with Rev. Liz Heller. His paintings were exhibited in the Westminster Gallery in 2005 and 2007.

The Martha Spencer Rogers Crèche Collection

A prime example of art that serves the Westminster Gallery's mission is the collection of 113 crèches from 79 countries donated by member Martha Spencer Rogers and displayed upstairs near the Sunday school rooms. Rev. Elizabeth Heller says, "I am so thrilled when I come in and I see a child telling an adult what their favorite crèche is in the cases. Every once in a while, I go up the hallway and just stand around waiting to hear someone talk about them."

Worship conducted with "dignity and joy, warmth and beauty" is the heart of Westminster's congregational life. Sermons are scripturally based, intelligent, and provocative, and the music is of high quality. The music and the Word seem to echo each other. Is it all serendipitous? Has God directly intervened to smooth out any jarring elements? Or could it be the Green Machine?

Word and music are fundamental to Westminster's Presbyterian worship, and every service originates in a conversation between the two. Pastor Tim Hart-Andersen and Minister of Music and the Arts Melanie Ohnstad sit down together for several full workdays during the summer to plan the church year. They begin by reading the Biblical texts aloud from the Lectionary and letting the texts suggest themes, sermon topics, liturgical elements, mood, musical styles, hymns, anthems. They emerge with a green notebook about half an inch thick that sketches out the church year from Coming Together Sunday through Pentecost. Ohnstad hosts a brunch at her house and invites the music staff to pore over the Green Machine and "parse out the Sundays" to decide, for example,

which are most suitable and practical for the youth choirs or the handbell choir or guest musicians. Then the Green Machine gets passed on to incorporate education programming.

The goal is not to put on an impeccable show but to create, in Choir Director Jere Lantz's words, "deep, meaningful worship." Beauty enhances depth and meaning.

"I experience God rationally, certainly," Ohnstad explains, "but very sensually as well through my ears and through my eyes. I see God in the beauty of nature, but also in poetry, story, architecture, and stained glass. I view music as a pathway—not a pathway—a boulevard to God. God is for me the source of beauty." Beauty also amplifies message. Lantz explains, "When people come to me and say, Hey, the choir sounded great today, I love it, but when people come to me and say, That was a great service. I really felt the message today, and the choir did its part to make that happen, that's the highest compliment."

>>>

Left to right: Minister of Music and the Arts Melanic Ohnstad and Choir Director Jere Lantz rehearse the choir. Lantz pauses before the service. Ohnstad at the organ console.

Unity and integrity in worship are time-honored ideals at Westminster, but the unified approach to planning that produced the Green Machine may be new. Two old tensions, between worship and performance and between the familiar and the new, still have to be negotiated. Westminster's leadership has long been cautious about letting worship stray into performance, even when only paid professionals sang in the choir. One measure of that caution is uncertainty about applause. In 1987 the Session asked Dr. Meisel to request that the congregation stay seated for the organ postlude and not applaud, lest the glory go to Ed Berryman rather than God. Thirteen years later Rev. Tim Hart-Andersen assured concerned elders that applause may also be a spontaneous expression of the power of the Spirit.

Jere Lantz has chosen to de-emphasize choral concerts and to pursue collaborations within a worshipful context, such as the Downtown Interfaith Choral Festival, which alternates years and church locations, and the biennial Presbytery Choral Festival held at Westminster. Even the choir's Christmas CD, "What a Wonder," was meant to instill the feeling of worship, "not high-falutin' arrangements, just the basic carols, sung in a very basic, straightforward way."

Twentieth-century Session minutes reveal periodic grumblings about new music and yearnings for old standards. As the Word invites us to leave our comfort zones and as Westminster diversifies and reaches out to the world, its musical repertoire necessarily grows. "The hymnal is so rich and represents a creating body, still creating," Ohnstad says. "The corpus of hymnody that is used on a regular basis, and that the congregation is coming to know and claim as its own, has really expanded in the last ten years."

World Communion Sunday and Pentecost are celebrations that include international music, often by guest musicians who bring authenticity to it. As music of other eras and cultures is introduced, the congregation learns new musical styles as well. Rather than hold to a "signature sound," Lantz trains the choir to honor the musical sensibility of the time and place in which the piece was composed. Sunday morning is not the only opportunity to widen the boulevard to God. The monthly Celtic service in the chapel reaches back to the ancient music of Scotland, a homeland of Presbyterianism, and Taizé worship on Lenten Wednesdays uses chants that suit the contemplative tone of the season.

Gourds and drums will not displace Bach or Isaac Watts. "We would be really remiss if we didn't continue to learn and teach the next generation the great works that have been created," Ohnstad believes. "Going forth into the future is kind of like this big glacier that keeps gaining more mass, and picking up more silt and soil and richness as it goes through the eons of time. I think that's what music in the church is like. It's just wonderful to be part of that."
✛

At left: Cantus, a male vocal ensemble that records and performs internationally, sings periodically in worship in exchange for using Westminster as its local rehearsal space.

At right from top: A 2003 children's choir is conducted by Barbara Harvey, director of early childhood music from 2002-07.

The local ensemble Excelsior leads congregational singing in celebration of Dr. Martin Luther King, Jr. Sunday in 2007.

The handbell choir, directed by Nancy Carter, opens the service.

THE CHILDREN AND YOUTH OF
WESTMINSTER TODAY

"I see God in the church through the relationships formed that cross normal boundaries of class or race or age, and also in the willingness to help and do social service. I see God at Westminster just through our general awareness of what's going on in the outside world and all the boundaries that no longer exist within the church because we all believe something: in a higher power that brings us all together." Lilli Johnson-Moffet, age 18

"The people at church are really nice, including the pastors, and I have learned a lot and I have friends here. We have really cool Sunday school teachers and really cool choir directors. I feel closest to God when I am in choir, because I like singing to God." Anna Kruskop, age 11

"I like to come to Westminster and hang out with friends. The jazz band is a great thing to do. Free food, obviously, and the sermons are really good. I like how Tim speaks, and the leaders are really good. Westminster is fun. It's different than any other church I have been to. It has character; some are just all the same. I like how they have the youth group and stuff like that. I think that everybody would enjoy doing stuff like that—people my age." Michael Janasz, age 17

"Westminster is my home away from home. I come here on Wednesdays and Sundays. Westminster is a place where you can come and you don't have to worry about being mocked or teased. That's the kind of stuff that might happen to you at school, and then you come here and all of a sudden it doesn't matter anymore. It's like this giant big family here at Westminster that everyone is a part of and they all treat you like you are a brother or sister to them." John Wasiluk, age 13

Far left: Frequently Westminster's youth put on full-length, costumed musical plays. "Malice in the Palace," performed in 2004, tells the story of Esther.

This page (from top to bottom):
Anna Northenscold *(large photo).*
Robbie Mitchell *(at right).*
Alison Winter.
Emily Cochrane, Eva Mitchell, Lilli Johnson-Moffet, and Cody Iacono help drywall a house on a high school mission trip to an area of Mississippi damaged by Hurricane Katrina.

""Well, I think Westminster is a great community to go to, and they make you feel comfortable. It's a great place to be joining God, and there are a lot of nice people who are very smart and know what to do. There are people who are really helpful to this church and I think God thanks them for doing that." Hadley Schuld, age 8

SOCIAL JUSTICE ADVOCACY

While Westminster has a proud history of outreach meant to undergird the city's welfare, the church has been guarded about taking stands on public policy. When it has done so, it has spoken in the pastor's voice. Rev. David Burrell campaigned for blue laws in the 1880s. Arnold Lowe urged the congregation to write letters supporting the Civil Rights Act of 1964. As fundamentalist churches have intervened in politics in recent years, congregations like Westminster's have grown bolder about addressing injustice.

On May 15, 2003, Session adopted a Social Justice Advocacy policy that allows Session itself to take positions on public issues. The Social Justice Ministry Team, chaired by Kitty Martin, initiated this move, and after three drafts, much discussion, and several church-wide listening sessions over a year and a half, the policy passed.

One concern raised was whether Session could speak for the membership of the church. It does not. Positions are taken in the name of the Session of Westminster Presbyterian Church. Individual members retain their freedom of conscience.

To answer questions about the propriety of mixing religion and politics, Rev. Douglas Mitchell explained that advocacy is a long Presbyterian tradition with a sound basis in Scripture. Isaiah 58:6-8 is but one example: "Is not this the fast that I choose: to loose the bonds of injustice, to undo the thongs of the yoke, to let the oppressed go free, and to break every yoke?"

As one experienced in talking "about the messy politics of social change and what that has to do with the Gospel," Rev. Mitchell stresses the dual nature of effective mission: "Any work around social justice has to include both meeting emergency direct needs and changing the system that requires people to beg to meet those needs. Just doing the politics or just doing the direct service is inadequate. You learn what changes need to be made by working with people in the midst of the crisis."

By summer 2006 Session had unanimously approved policy positions on firearms and gun violence and on affordable housing. The Social Justice team had not expected firearms to be the premier issue, but because the state legislature was discussing how its proposed permit-to-carry law would apply to churches, Session decided to respond. Guy Mueller of the Social Justice team drove to St. Paul to deliver the firearms policy, fresh off the copy machine, to key legislators. His enthusiasm didn't persuade enough of them to oppose the bill, but Westminster can at least post signs banning guns on its premises. More action waits. "We Presbyterians like to do things in an orderly fashion and make sure everyone is heard," Sandy Wolfe Wood explains, "so we are sometimes behind the curve on some more controversial issues." Having petitions in support of gun control available at the Sunday coffee hour is an orderly effort.

Progress on housing has been more tangible. Session passed its first endorsement of specific legislation in January 2007 in favor of the Housing Solutions Act, an affordable housing bill in the legislature. As new co-owners of an affordably priced apartment building, members of Westminster and Plymouth Congregational Church have discussed tax and zoning policies with city and county officials.

The Social Justice Ministry Team seeks to engage more members of the congregation in advocacy. "There seems to be no lack of interest in doing hands-on mission activities," Wolfe Wood notes, "but gathering individuals to pursue advocacy, activism, and developing church policy presents some challenges. Policy change is less immediately rewarding than painting someone's house; it takes time and hours of dialogue to build a constituency of people willing to make something happen. But the results are longer-lasting." ✛

The Presbyterian Church (USA) has established a long record of taking stands and speaking out on issues related to justice in society. Westminster Presbyterian Church's actions are informed by this history. Just as Westminster has spoken out on issues of concern within the denomination, Westminster needs to use its voice to lead in the public sphere.

Westminster's policy paper on Social Justice Advocacy, adopted May 15, 2003

Social justice advocacy policies adopted by the Session of Westminster Presbyterian Church:

Policy on Taking Policy Positions
Adopted May 2003

Policy on Firearms and Gun Violence
Adopted October 2004

Policy on Housing and Inclusive Communities
Adopted June 2006

Sponsor of Housing Solutions Act
Signed January 2007

Westminster members and friends join hands in "Peace Across the Northside," May 2007. *Left to right:* Iris Pahlberg Peterson, Gretchen Musicant, Terry Skally, Doug Mitchell, and Lynda Stewart. This is an annual vigil held to show solidarity with North Minneapolis neighborhoods and with community groups working to end gun violence.

WESTMINSTER'S HOUSING MINISTRY

A special meeting of the congregation at 5:00 p.m. on Tuesday, April 25, 1978, authorized the Trustees to sell the Royal Apartments at 1821 First Avenue South, bequeathed to Westminster four years earlier. The reasons given for the sale were problems with tenants, a mere break-even cash flow, and the need to buy high-risk insurance. If only some prescient member had been there to interject, Wait! We will want that building thirty years from now!

In 2006 in anticipation of their Sesquicentennials the next year, Westminster and Plymouth Congregational Church joined with the Plymouth Church Neighborhood Foundation to create the Housing 150 Initiative to preserve and develop affordable housing in Minneapolis. Its first project was the purchase, repair, and updating of a twenty-one-unit apartment building at 1801 First Avenue South, renamed Abbott View in honor of Westminster's former hospital building across Eighteenth Street. A pending condominium conversion had threatened to displace the current tenants, people on fixed incomes supported by Section 8 housing subsidies.

Westminster's first enduring effort to shelter neighbors in need dates to 1986 when the Deacons inaugurated the Transitional Housing program. Its intent was to find clean, safe, affordable housing for people coming out of crises who could likely become self-supporting, such as domestically abused women and their children. Two early lessons shaped the program for the future: The typical client has other needs in addition to housing. And partnership with an existing, experienced agency is more effective than reinventing the wheel. The program has contracted with Episcopal Community Services for most of its life.

Transitional Housing requires a weekly, face-to-face, six-month or longer commitment from individual Westminster volunteers. Eric Adams, who has worked with the program since 1993, describes these volunteers as "part mentor, part friend, part >>>

Kathryn Anonsen participates in the annual Paint-a-thon, which spruces up homes of elderly and disabled people in the metropolitan area. The blue paint says it's 2005.

Far left: Doug Mitchell and Richard Nutt exercise their carpentry skills for Habitat for Humanity.

At left: A Habitat family.

Below: The steering committee that brought Housing 150's first project to fruition. The group includes representatives of Westminster, Plymouth Congregational Church, and the Plymouth Neighborhood Foundation.

>>>

listening board" in a "three-legged partnership with the client, the volunteer, and a professional case manager." The program transforms lives, and not only the clients'. "You are never quite the same after you've done this," Adams says. Transitional Housing's many success stories have inspired other churches to adopt Westminster's partnership model.

Individual members have volunteered with Habitat for Humanity since its arrival in the Twin Cities in 1985. The Mission Component of the capital campaign conducted in the late 1990s allowed the church to make a major contribution to Habitat. Westminster has joined with Congregations Building Community, a coalition of twenty downtown congregations, to help finance and build fifty-five homes in Heritage Park on the Near Northside, the former site of a controversial public housing project. Money and labor have been supplemented by diplomacy to make the new housing and its occupants welcome in the neighborhood.

The Housing 150 Initiative follows a significant turn in how Westminster interprets the charge in Isaiah 58:7 to "share your bread with the hungry and shelter the homeless poor." In May 2003 Session approved a policy on Social Justice Advocacy that informs the church's response to human suffering. Applying the Social Justice Advocacy policy to housing needs, Session in June 2006 adopted a policy position on affordable housing that includes this statement:

"Our vision is for a compassionate and equitable distribution of affordable housing resources throughout our metropolitan region such that no one is required to pay more than 30 percent of income for housing."

In addition to buying and building such housing, Westminster works with organizations like MICAH that pursue changes in home financing, zoning regulations, and other policies and practices that keep our neighbors homeless, inadequately housed, or financially overwhelmed.

For Associate Pastor Doug Mitchell, getting to work on housing means returning to a youthful love. As an undergraduate at Auburn University in Alabama in the 1960s and a member of Westminster Fellowship, he helped found a small non-profit that repaired houses in nearby rural African American communities. As our minister for Faith in Action, he invites the congregation to contribute to Westminster's housing mission, whether by the stroke of a hammer, a signature on a check, moral support to someone applying for a loan, or a lobbying visit at the legislature. ✚

Local partnerships
KWANZAA CHURCH AND FAMILIA DE FÉ

Westminster has long been committed to planting new churches and to recycling used church buildings when neighborhood demographics change. In 1994 the Presbytery of the Twin Cities Area conceived the idea to organize an Afrocentric church in the former Highland Park Presbyterian Church at 2100 Emerson Avenue North. After discussions that involved Westminster as a potential mission partner, Presbytery submitted a proposal to General Assembly's Mission Development Resource Committee. The proposal was accepted with the contingency that sufficient funds be raised to make the church viable. Westminster underwrote the start-up and recruited other churches as funding partners. The Reverends Alika and Ralph Galloway were called in 1997 to serve as co-pastors. Kwanzaa Community Presbyterian Church held its first worship service in January 1998 and received its charter in February 2002.

Under the Galloways' guidance and with active lay leadership, Kwanzaa Church has become a beacon of hope in a neighborhood plagued by poverty, the drug trade, and gang violence. Among its foundational scriptures is this verse from Psalm 33: "How good and pleasant it is when God's people live together in peace!" Kwanzaa's outreach efforts, particularly through its Nia-Imani Youth and Family Development Center, intend to strengthen families and counter youth violence. The church also conducts an HIV/AIDS ministry that is culturally and economically suited to its population. As Westminster's Associate Pastor Doug Mitchell explains, "When you are dealing with AIDS and a low-income community you have got to deal with issues like keeping utilities on. If you've got no electricity you can't keep your meds."

Westminster has continued to work in partnership with Kwanzaa's congregation, not only as a donor, but with joint women's groups and Bible study, a shared transitional housing project, the HIV/AIDS ministry, pulpit exchanges, internship opportunities for Kwanzaa seminarians, and fellowship. Westminster member Amy Crary says of the partnership, "It has been really rewarding. They are a very energetic group of people."

On a bittersweet note, the aging congregation at Calvary Presbyterian Church has recently vacated its building at 3700 Bryant Avenue North. Kwanzaa has acquired the site and will eventually move its worship, its HIV/AIDS ministry, and other programs there, leaving the Emerson building available for the Nia-Imani Center.

Westminster has begun a somewhat similar relationship with Familia de Fé (Family of Faith), the Presbytery's Hispanic new church development located in the former House of Faith Presbyterian Church at 668 Broadway Street in Northeast Minneapolis. Westminster's Associate Pastor Annika Lister Stroope served on the pastor nominating committee that called the Reverend Walter Chuquimia. On World Communion Sunday in October 2006, Rev. Chuquimia and his founding congregation participated in worship at Westminster. ✦

Above: Co-pastors Ralph and Alika Galloway pose in front of Kwanzaa Church after the Sunday service while their congregation files out of the sanctuary.

Who is my neighbor?

WEST AFRICAN IMMIGRANTS

Back in 1980 a young man from a prominent family in Kumba, Cameroon, moved to Minneapolis to pursue a college education. A friend living here already had recommended the University of Minnesota. He settled in among other immigrants in Cedar-Riverside and accompanied his friend to a Baptist church on Sundays. But one day the bus he was riding passed a large Presbyterian church on Nicollet Avenue. His father had been active with the Basel Mission, a Swiss Presbyterian mission that led to the independent Presbyterian Church in Cameroon. "The next Sunday I rode the bus downtown and attended church and I listened to Dr. Meisel preach," Joseph Mukete remembers. "I said to myself, This is where I belong."

The next year three young sisters from a Ghanaian family named Ablorh were baptized at Westminster. Six months later Agnes Mbong transferred in from a Presbyterian church in Cameroon. From these quiet beginnings, a community has grown, mostly by word of mouth, and helped to diversify and revitalize Westminster's congregation. Some of the church's West African members come from Ghana, Nigeria, and Liberia, but most are from Cameroon and Togo. They emigrated for reasons that should sound familiar to European Americans who have traced their own ancestry: Because they wanted a better education than they could get at home. Because an economic downturn made sustaining a good living difficult. Because power was concentrated in the hands of a group that didn't look favorably on their kind. >>>

The Right Reverend Nyansako-ni-Nku, the Moderator of the Presbyterian Church of Cameroon and President of the All-Africa Conference of Churches, visited the Twin Cities in 2005. Here guests from Arlington Hills Presbyterian Church in St. Paul join Westminster members in the Meisel Room for a blessing of the newly formed U.S. branch of the Christian Women's Fellowship of the Presbyterian Church in Cameroon. The women in yellow are full members of the Fellowship, and the women in blue are members-in-training.

Eugene Fotso, a Cameroonian American, teaches the fifth and sixth grades in Sunday school. David Leighton listens intently.

>>>

They wound up in the Twin Cities for familiar reasons, too:

A scholarship. A job. The encouragement of friends and relatives who had come before. Or, like Ama Sabah, they fell in love with a countryman who now called Minnesota home.

The Africans in church on Sundays are not the whole of Westminster's African community. Newer arrivals often hold jobs that require Sunday work. West African members serve on Session and the Board of Deacons and in places of usefulness throughout the church. The women stand out in their colorful, patterned clothes and headdresses. Ama Sabah, from Togo, explains, "It matters to me that I am African, an integral part of Westminster, which comprises a blend of different people, different cultures, and different styles. I get a lot of inquiries from people about my clothes. Having a different dress style is a way of claiming my heritage. Their colorfulness is also an asset; it makes people want to learn more."

In its earlier association with immigrants, notably the Chinese and Scandinavians, Westminster members felt obliged to convert them to a proper Christian morality and American habits. With the West Africans evangelism can work the other way. Most are Presbyterians already, and they tend to be more Biblically literate and more comfortable speaking a language of faith than their U.S.-born pew mates. They bring with them forms of worship that challenge Westminster's European-derived decorum. "The Presbyterian Church here is very conservative," Ama Sabah says. "Back home we dance during the praise and worship ministry, and the preaching . . . is more vibrant. The pastor actually has a conversation with the church attendants rather than a lecture." An African choir directed by Melissa Nambangi from Cameroon has introduced more staid churchgoers to call-and-response singing and ululation.

One benefit the West African members have brought is a renewed international mission. Unlike the colonial style of foreign mission, Westminster's alliance with the Presbyterian Church in Cameroon, which Joseph Mukete helped establish, is a partnership. Material goods and medical technology flow, to be sure, from the rich United States to poorer Cameroon, but members who have traveled to Cameroon return with inspiration, new understanding, and a strengthened faith. "For the experienced members of Westminster," Mukete says, "this has given them an enormous experience with the way people worship in a different part of the world. I remember one of the members said, 'I've never seen a people who have so very little yet whose spirits remain high.' That is what you will see in Cameroon."

Ama Sabah hopes for similar partnerships in other African nations. Her dream is to open an orphanage in Togo and to help children "either infected or affected by HIV." ✛

Something really useful THE RED SHIRT MISSION

Above: John Murray at work in Kenya.
Below left: Anne Murray holds a Kenyan child.
Below: A red shirt.

The Red Shirt offering has been collected for so many years that few in the congregation may remember its origin. In 1970 when Anne Murray and her husband, John, a cardiologist at the University of Minnesota, told their three youngest children John's plans to spend his sabbatical in South Africa writing a cardiology textbook, the children responded skeptically:

Why not do something really useful, Dad?

Dr. Murray never wrote the book. Instead, the Murrays traveled to Niger where the whole family restored an abandoned hospital. Even twelve-year-old Christopher was put to work managing the dispensary. They returned to Africa yearly after that and were eventually invited to set up a mobile medical mission among the Maasai in Kenya. Some of the respiratory illnesses they treated could be attributed to cold nights in the high-altitude terrain. A supply of blankets was obtained for the children with pneumonia. The Red Shirt part of the mission began the next summer after the Murrays discovered the blankets adorning the tall Maasai men. Anne decided they needed to give the children some article of clothing that the men could not fit into. Back home at Westminster, Lola Barnes designed a simple shirt in red, an important color to the Maasai. Volunteers have sewn thousands of these garments for distribution in Kenya. A *National Geographic* feature article on the Maasai even caught a few red shirts in its photographs. Well into their eighties now, the Murrays continue to make the yearly trip. ✚

The church's first global partnership had a casual beginning. Rev. Dan Little, pastor-in-residence, agreed in 1998 to host a visit by the Reverend João Dias, dean of a Brazilian seminary called ITEBA (Institute for Theological Education in Bahia) located in the city of Salvador. His friends Bill and June Rogers had served there as PCUSA mission co-workers and wanted help shoring up support for the unique school. The Reverend John Sinclair, a retired synod administrator deeply experienced in Latin American mission who worships at Westminster, knew Dias and helped arrange the visit. Four years later Session signed a five-year covenant with the seminary, becoming one of about a dozen PCUSA churches in the ITEBA Network.

ITEBA was started by several Presbyterian ministers expelled from their conservative denomination in the 1960s for resisting Brazil's military junta. The school, now ecumenical, focuses on preparing Afro-Brazilians, particularly women, to work with the poor of Salvador. While some students go on to church ministry, most become activists and advocates, service providers and social workers for the masses of impoverished Afro-Brazilians in the northeast region of Brazil.

Westminster helps fund ITEBA with an annual pledge and special campaigns. Several teams from the congregation have visited the seminary and participated in the *Mutirao*, two weeks of work and study with network participants from across the United States. Visitors from ITEBA have come to Minneapolis to share their faith with our congregation.

An additional partnership in Salvador got underway in 2007 with a Presbyterian congregation called Itapagipe that is closely connected to the seminary. Vince Thomas, part of the team that helped arrange the new partnership, keeps a photo on his desk of an Afro-Brazilian girl named Amanda who is the same age as his daughter, Mary. Having seen the poverty in Salvador first-hand, he says, "We can no longer pretend that we are somehow living life at a higher level, detached from all of that." ✢

Center: Westminster global partners Reid MacDonald, Tim Hart-Andersen, and Vince Thomas pose with Sandra Santos, a faculty member at the ITEBA seminary, and Marlene Moreira da Silva, the academic director. *Left and right:* Details from a painting by the Brazilian artist Kiko Veloso.

Global partnership CUBA

Below: The Versalles Church in Matanzas, Cuba.

Westminster's new pastor, Tim Hart-Andersen, brought with him a love of Latin America. He had traveled and studied extensively in the region, including a trip to Cuba in 1982. When he heard that a Westminster couple, Bob Kriel and Linda Krach, had recently traveled to Cuba, he suggested that the church consider establishing a partnership with a congregation on the island.

An exploratory trip by several Westminster members in 2002 resulted in a covenant of partnership with the Iglesia Presbiteriana El Redentor in the city of Matanzas. The church, locally called Versalles after its neighborhood, has welcomed Westminster teams nearly every year since then, including a choir formed for the purpose and decked out in colorful Lands' End® polo shirts. Those who travel to Matanzas grow especially fond of the Reverend Carlos Piedra and his wife, Mercedes Herrera, who has, in turn, visited Westminster.

The covenant signed by the sessions of both churches makes it clear that the primary purpose of the relationship is Christian solidarity. The congregations have established a prayer partnership, in which families pray for each other regularly, and they stay in touch as best they can, given the restrictions on communication between citizens of the two countries. Another partnership covenant with the national Presbyterian Church in Cuba allows Westminster to offer financial support to the entire church on the island. The Cuban synod decides where the funds are needed most urgently.

A group of college students from Westminster took a life-changing trip to Cuba in 2005. Kat Nichols, then the coordinator of youth ministries, comments, "You could almost see their demeanor change, see them thinking a lot deeper. It was the excitement about getting to go to Cuba, but then God working in them during that time. It led to some very deep, thick conversations with a couple of the students in particular that have led them to reconsider their majors in college and what they want to do." ✛

Because Westminster is home to scores of African, mostly Cameroonian, immigrants, Cameroon seemed a natural place to seek a partnership. Joseph Mukete had already opened the doors by arranging to send communion silver and choir robes from Westminster's collection to his hometown church in Kumba.

Rev. Doug Mitchell led a team to Cameroon in 2004 to explore a formal partnership with a congregation of the Presbyterian Church in Cameroon (PCC). Later that year Session signed a covenant with the three-thousand-member Kumba Town Presbyterian Church similar to those with churches in Cuba and Brazil. The five-year covenant invites the two congregations to be in Christian solidarity with each other, exchanging prayers, worship, study, and church life.

Westminster also partners with AIDS CareLink, a medical ministry in Douala, Cameroon. Teams of health care professionals from the congregation have traveled there to work under the direction of Dr. Sam Ngwane, and the church has made a long-term financial commitment to improving health care. Psychiatrist John Heefner describes his time in Cameroon as "a sobering experience. We were seeing people being treated for schizophrenia who were on drugs that we no longer use here because the side effects are so bad. They can't afford the new drugs. In this particular city there is one psychiatrist for about two million people."

The PCC challenged Westminster in 2004 to help the African church both confront the AIDS crisis and help prepare ministers. One response was a significant five-year financial commitment as part of the PCUSA's Mission Initiative campaign. The denomination called the Reverend Shirley Hill, a registered nurse, and Westminster commissioned her in 2006 to serve alongside the PCC developing AIDS prevention and testing programs. Cameroon is, coincidentally, where Rev. Arnold Lowe, Westminster's pastor from 1941-65, began his ministry as a missionary. His daughter, Mary Lee Dayton, still an active member of the church, addressed the second part of the challenge with a substantial gift to establish the Westminster Presbyterian Church, Minneapolis, Academic Excellence Fund at the Presbyterian Theological Seminary in Kumba, Cameroon. ✢

The youth choir of the Primary School operated by Westminster's partner congregation, the Kumba Town Presbyterian Church, Kumba, Cameroon.

COMING FULL CIRCLE IN CAMEROON

by Timothy Hart-Andersen

When I arrived at Westminster in 1999, I was delighted that the pastor emeritus, Donald M. Meisel, still participated fully in the life of the church. I was surprised, however, to find myself laboring in the shadow of Arnold Lowe, who retired in 1965! There is a mystique about Lowe. As we began planning Westminster's 150th Anniversary, I determined to learn more.

In 2005 I visited the archives of the Presbyterian Historical Society in Philadelphia to look into Dr. Lowe's missionary service in Cameroon. In century-old records, I met the twenty-two-year-old Lowe, transplanted from Switzerland, studying at Bloomfield Academy in New Jersey. There, in 1910, he met a Presbyterian missionary looking for young men who spoke German to come to Africa. "Somehow I felt the hand of God was upon me," Lowe wrote. "I pledged myself to go."

His application was rebuffed twice. Why would the Board of Foreign Missions spurn a man in vigorous health, full of zeal, and fluent in the language of the African colony where he would serve? Perhaps it was his Jewish roots. His supporters argued with eloquence that the earnest "young Israelite" was of thoroughly Christian character. "The only disqualification," one of them asserted, "would be that the honorable Board would not take a converted Jew!" Lowe had come into contact with Christian life at nineteen, under the guidance of the Reverend H. Frank. "As a love in God's hand, I was converted," he wrote.

His entreaties eventually convinced the skeptical board, and he sailed for Africa in June 1912. He later referred to his time in Cameroon as "the happiest years of my life." After two years there Lowe was posted to the American mission at Batanga, near Kribi.

Somehow I felt the hand of God was upon me," Lowe wrote. "I pledged myself to go."

His oratorical skill, fervent faith, and fluency in local languages made him a potent presence.

When World War I broke out, French naval forces attacked Cameroon. The Americans withdrew their missionaries, except for the head of the Batanga mission, Dr. Albert Adams, his wife, and Arnold Lowe. They stayed on for several difficult months in the middle of a war zone.

The mission station became an oasis for Cameroonians; more than a thousand sought protection there. Soldiers beat Lowe for impeding their search for suspected partisans. The German defeat at Kribi abruptly ended Lowe's missionary career. The French commander accused him of spying for the Germans and expelled him in early 1915. Twenty-six years later as another world war was raging, Westminster called Lowe as pastor. Little was known of his experience in Africa; nothing was known of his Jewish origins until the records in the Presbyterian Historical Society were opened and read. >>>

>>>

A year after my trip to Philadelphia I led a team from Westminster to Cameroon to visit our partner church in Kumba and to search for the old mission compound in Batanga. Betsy Dovydenas, a granddaughter of Lowe, accompanied us, as did the Reverend Beth Hart-Andersen, my wife, and Joseph Mukete, a Westminster elder from Cameroon.

On our way through Kribi we stopped at a brightly painted Presbyterian Church. An older gentleman listened as we told him in halting French about our former minister, Betsy's *grand-père*, a long-ago missionary. Smiling, he motioned for us to follow and led us behind the church and down a dirt road to a house where two women sat on the porch reading scripture. As Betsy told them about her grandfather, a look of recognition passed across the older woman's face. She found a photo of her adoptive mother, Evelyn Alice Adams, daughter of Dr. and Mrs. Albert Adams, who had worked with Arnold Lowe in Batanga nearly a century ago. The two missionary granddaughters embraced with joy!

The next day our team made its way to the former mission compound, guided by our new Cameroonian friends. A machete-wielding young man cut through the jungle to the overgrown ruins of the chapel and house where Lowe and the Adamses had lived and served. Standing in the clearing, I read words Lowe had written about being called to serve God. We gave thanks to God for Arnold Lowe's ministry there, for the continuing witness of the Cameroonian church, and for God's providence that had brought us together.

Our visit had another purpose. The archival records show that in 1914 Lowe and other American missionaries laid out a dream for Cameroon: to create a seminary to prepare Africans for the ministry. World War I cut their dream short. Ninety-two years later, as part of the church's 150th Anniversary Campaign, Lowe's daughter and Westminster member Mary Lee Dayton created and endowed the Westminster Academic Excellence Fund at Kumba Theological Seminary.

At the seminary I talked about Arnold Lowe, his dedication to God's work in Cameroon, and his beloved congregation in Minneapolis. Betsy read a statement from her mother, Mary Lee: "With this gift, Westminster and my family come full circle, back to Cameroon, to reestablish ties made long ago. We give thanks to God for making this possible."

Thus is the future tied to the past, as Westminster builds on a partnership newly established but echoing historic connections. Arnold Lowe's pledge to go to Africa was fulfilled not once, but twice, as the congregation he served takes up where he left off.

Being part of completing the circle was a blessing for me. If I do nothing else in my ministry, this will have been enough—to link a family with its past, to bridge a church's historic and ongoing commitments, and to have witnessed the love of God at work around the world. +

Thanks be to God for these stories, and for the hundreds like them—stories of those who have worshiped and served God over the years at Westminster Presbyterian Church, whose doors are flung open to the world, that the love of Jesus might enter in and go forth.

IMAGE CREDITS

Credits are listed by page number; name of image (if more than one image appears per page); photographer or artist (if known); source.

i Both, Hennepin History Museum

iii Susan Gilmore

v Charles J. Hibbard, Minnesota Historical Society

vi Doug Knutson

1 Hennepin History Museum

2 Hennepin History Museum

3 Edward A. Bromley, Minneapolis Public Library

4 Edward A. Bromley, Minneapolis Public Library

5 Church, Minnesota Historical Society

Portrait, WPC archives

6 Hennepin History Museum

7 Portrait, Minnesota Historical Society

Notes, WPC archives

8 Jonathan Edwards Center, Yale University

9 Benjamin Franklin Upton, Minnesota Historical Society

10 Church interior, WPC archives

Hand fan, Susan Gilmore, WPC archives

11 Map, Hennepin History Museum

Portrait, WPC archives

12 Escapees, Adrian J.Ebell, Minnesota Historical Society

Portrait,Nicollet County Historical Society, St. Peter, MN

13 WPC archives

14 Edward A. Bromley, Minneapolis Public Library

15 Portrait, Presbyterian Historical Society, Philadelphia, PA

Sermon, Minnesota Historical Society

16 Darwin, Mary Evans Picture Library

Sermon, Minnesota Historical Society

17 Minneapolis Public Library

18 Minneapolis Public Library

19 Washburn Mill, Edward A. Bromley, Minneapolis Public Library

20 Artist rendering, Jacoby, Minneapolis Public Library

7th Street Church, *Minneapolis Star Journal,* WPC archives

Church lithograph, WPC archives

21 Engravings, WPC archives

22 Susan Gilmore, WPC archives

23 Pews, George Heinrich

Pew receipt, WPC archives

24 Hymnal, John Lauenstein and Susan Gilmore, WPC archives

25 WPC archives

26 Both, WPC archives

27 Hennepin History Museum

28 WPC archives

29 Both, WPC archives

30 Portrait, WPC archives

Stained glass window, George Heinrich

31 WPC archives

32 Women, Bing Wong, Minnesota Historical Society

Chinese Hymnal, Minnesota Historical Society

33 Yee Sing Woo, Acme Advertising Co., Minnesota Historical Society

Tsui and children, WPC archives

34 Hennepin History Museum

35 Both, Hennepin History Museum

Diary quote, Minneapolis Public Library, Special Collections

36 Both, Hennepin History Museum

37 Offering envelope, WPC archives

38 Temperance, WPC archives

Wood relief, Peter Wedin, Minnesota Historical Society

39 Bohemian Flats, George E. Luxton, Minnesota Historical Society

Map, Hennepin History Museum

40 Riverside, Hennepin History Museum

Flyer, WPC archives

41 Portrait, courtesy of Phyllis Paul

42 WPC exterior boarded up, Hennepin History Museum

12th street exterior, Venning P. Hollis, Minnesota Historical Society

Map, Hennepin History Museum

43 WPC archives

44 Both, WPC archives

45 WPC archives

46 Portrait, WPC archives

47 Church interior photographed by Sweet, Minnesota Historical Society

Church exterior, William Gary Purcell, University of Minnesota Libraries, Northwest Architectural Archives

48 Exterior, Minnesota Historical Society

Portrait, WPC archives

49 Hennepin History Museum

50 Taft, Minnesota Historical Society

Women, scrapbook of Herman and Ann Maclean Johnson, courtesy of Bruce M. Jones

51 Diary quote, Minneapolis Public Library, Special Collections

Youth group, Hennepin History Museum

52 Roger Woo

53 WPC archives

54 Cartoon, *Boston Post,* January 29, 1909

55 Rich Photo Services, WPC archives

56 Men in circle, Roger Woo

Picnic, John and Laura Hawkins

57 Portrait, WPC archives

Stained glass window, George Heinrich

58 Scrapbook of Herman and Ann Maclean Johnson, courtesy of Bruce M. Jones

59 WPC archives

60 Abbott photographs, WPC archives

61 Minnesota Historical Society

62 Norton & Peel, Minnesota Historical Society

63 WPC archives

64-65 Red Cross, WPC archives

Letter, WPC archives

66 Presbyterian Historical Society, Philadelphia, PA

67 Shell of a church,Presbyterian Historical Society, Philadelphia, PA

Two photographs of Lebanon, WPC archives

68 Presbyterian Historical Society, Philadelphia, PA

69 Letter, Presbyterian Historical Society, Philadelphia, PA

Offering envelope, WPC archives

70 Youth, scrapbook of Herman and Ann Maclean Johnson,courtesy of Bruce M. Jones

Maude Royden, from the magazine *Sketch,* 10 August 1922

71 William Jennings Bryan, *Seven Questions in Dispute* (New York, 1924)

72 WPC archives

73 Breadline, Charles Hibbard, Minnesota Historical Society

Portrait, WPC archives

74 Union City Mission, A.F. Raymond, Minnesota Historical Society

Veterans Memorial Day Parade, Minneapolis Public Library

75 Minneapolis Public Library

76 With permission from the Dayton family

77 Susan Gilmore

78 With permission from the Dayton family

79 Troop 33, Roger Woo

Girl scouts, Norton & Peel,

80 Scouts in dining room, Roger Woo

Dave Moore with scouts, Paul Irmiter

81 Both, Roger Woo

82 All photographs, WPC archives

83 WPC archives

84 Roger Woo

85 Roger Woo

86 Communion, Roger Woo

Street scene, Norton & Peel

88 Chuck Haga

89 WPC archives

90 Roger Woo

91 Letters, WPC archives

92 WPC archives

93 Both, Roger Woo

94 Doug Knutson

95 Peace march, Minnesota Historical Society

Meeting, Roger Woo

96 Bates, Roger Woo

Bus, Norton & Peel

97 Roger Woo

98 *St. Paul Pioneer Press*, Minnesota Historical Society

99 Office, WPC archives

Al and Sharon Cooper, Sam Cooke

100 Courtesy of Cheri Register

101 WPC archives

102 Left, courtesy of Liz Heller

Center, WPC archives

Right, Sam Cooke

104 WPC archives

105 Hmong scouts, courtesy of the *Star Tribune*

Painting, Cy Thao, The Westminster Collection

107 WPC archives

108 Susan Gilmore

109 WPC archives

110 Left and center, WPC archives

Right, Susan Gilmore

111 Chuck Haga

112 Doug Knutson

113 Chuck Haga

114 Both, Doug Knutson

115 George Heinrich

116 Stained glass, George Heinrich

Portrait, provided by the family of Phyllis Sutton

117 Children by tree, Roger Woo

Girls, WPC archives

118 John and Laura Hawkins

119 WPC archives

120 Great Hall, Dan Marshall

Liz Heller, Roger Woo

121 Heller Commons, WPC archives

Cup, Sandy Wolfe Wood

122 Sam Cooke

123 Roger Woo

Diary quote, Minneapolis Public Library, Special Collections

124 WPC archives

125 Meisel with children, Roger Woo

Strandin, WPC archives

126 Left, Roger Woo

Right, WPC archives

127 Tim and children, Dan Marshall

Mister Rogers, used with permission by Family Communications

128 Top and center, Roger Woo

Lower, courtesy of the Zapchenk family

129 Dan Marshall

130 Susan Gilmore

131 WPC archives

132 Sam Cooke

133 Joe Carlson

134 WPC archives

135 Jeff Krueger

136 Pipes, WPC archives

Interior, Jeff Krueger

137 Interior, Joe Carlson

Dan Little, Sam Cooke

138 Aerial, Sam Cooke

Great Hall, Joe Carlson

139 Aerial, Cho, Myoung Hwan

Cornerstone, Doug Knutson

140 Susan Gilmore

141 Top, Susan Gilmore

Exterior, George Heinrich

142 Sam Cooke

143 Dan Marshall

144 Tiles, photographed by George Heinrich

Granlund sculpture, Rodney Allen Schwartz

Heller and Schwartz, Susan Gilmore

145 George Heinrich

146 Painting, The Westminster Collection, Susan Gilmore

Crèche, The Martha Spencer Rogers Creche Collection

147 Left, Dan Marshall

Center, Sam Cooke

Right, WPC archives

148 Susan Gilmore

149 Top, Alan Touchberry

Center, Susan Gilmore

Lower, Doug Knutson

150 Alan Touchberry

151 Anna Northenscold, Dan Marshall

Robbie Mitchell, Doug Knutson

Alison Winter, Dan Marshall

Youth group, WPC archives

153 Susan Gilmore

154 WPC archives

155 Abbott View, Sam Cooke

Both Habitat for Humanity, WPC archives

156 Susan Gilmore

157 Rodney Allen Schwartz

158 Dan Marshall

159 Both John and Anne Murray, WPC archives

Red shirt, Susan Gilmore, WPC archives

160 Painting, courtesy of Doug Mitchell

Group in Brazil, courtesy of Vince Thomas

161 Rodney Allen Schwartz

162 Patrice Paton

163 Presbyterian Historical Society, Philadelphia, PA

164 Patrice Paton

165 Courtesy of M.A. Mortenson Company

168 Stained glass, George Heinrich

Front Cover
Susan Gilmore

Back Cover
Susan Gilmore

The History Book Team

Anniversary committee liaison: **Trish Van Pilsum**
Archival assistance: **Sandra Berthene, Rodney Allen Schwartz**
Clergy liaison: **Rev. Timothy Hart-Andersen**
Design and layout: **Sandy Wolfe Wood**
Editing: **Sandra Berthene, D'Arlyn Marks, Cheri Register**
Historic image restoration and digital processing: **John Lauenstein**
Oral history project management: **Bruce Jones, Peggy Tillitt**
Photography and photo research: **Susan Gilmore**
Printing: **Craig Johnson, Shearson Publishing, Inc.**
Project management: **D'Arlyn Marks**
Research and writing: **Jacqueline R. deVries, Cheri Register**
Staff support: **Kathy Fisher**

Interviewers: Sandra Berthene, Karen Collier, Jane Cooper,
Jacqueline R. deVries, Dan Franklin, Marian Hoffman, Bruce Jones,
Martha Karels, Barbara LaValleur, D'Arlyn Marks, Barbara Mauk,
Nancy Morin, Beth Patten, Cheri Register, John Sinclair, CC Strom,
Peggy Tillitt, Cindy Weldon
Transcribers: Sandra Berthene, Janice Ditzler, Judith Harper,
Ralph Watkins, Cindy Weldon

Thank you to the staffs of the American Swedish Institute, Big Spring
Presbyterian Church in Newville, PA, the Hennepin History Museum,
Macalester College Library, the Minneapolis Public Library Special
Collections, the Minnesota Historical Society, the Presbyterian
Historical Society in Philadelphia, and to John Ankeny, Phyllis Paul,
and Wendy Williamson for access to private collections.